NEW YORK

CROSSWORDS

50 Big Puzzles

BY CATHY ALLIS

Simon & Schuster

NEW YORK   LONDON   TORONTO   SYDNEY   NEW DELHI

Simon & Schuster
1230 Avenue of the Americas
New York, NY 10020

First Simon & Schuster trade paperback edition June 2019

SIMON & SCHUSTER and colophon are registered trademarks
of Simon & Schuster, Inc.

For information about special discounts for bulk purchases, please contact
Simon & Schuster Special Sales at 1-866-506-1949
or business@simonandschuster.com.

The Simon & Schuster Speakers Bureau can bring authors to your
live event. For more information or to book an event, contact
the Simon & Schuster Speakers Bureau at 1-866-248-3049
or visit our website at www.simonspeakers.com.

Manufactured in the United States of America

5   7   9   10   8   6   4

Library of Congress Cataloging-in-Publication Data is available.

ISBN 978-1-9821-0655-3

Introduction

In the beginning, *New York* magazine did not have its own crossword puzzle. When *New York* first appeared in 1963, as the Sunday magazine section of the *New York Herald Tribune,* it instead reprinted a crossword from the *Times* of London, a fiercely difficult, often-impenetrable-for-Americans puzzle in the British cryptic style. (It even appeared beneath the rubric "WORLD'S MOST CHALLENGING CROSSWORD.") That puzzle, and its title, may have been great for the brand—implying that the *Trib* had the smartest readers in town—but one seriously doubts that it was solved or loved by a wide swath of New Yorkers.

In the five decades since, that's all changed. The *Herald Tribune* went out of business in 1966, and *New York* was reincarnated as a weekly glossy magazine two years later. Its puzzles have gone from mostly ignored to widely beloved, ranging from fiendish to accessible. From April to December 1968, the composer and lyricist Stephen Sondheim contributed a cryptic crossword to each issue, usually with an extra layer of complexity on top of the basic across-and-down-style grid. The next year, when he gave up the gig, Mary Ann Madden's wordplay contests began to alternate with crosswords by Richard Maltby. The *Times* of London puzzle continued to appear in *New York* for many years as well.

The tradition continued. When *New York* absorbed *Cue* magazine in 1980, it picked up the friendly, quirky American-style crosswords of Maura B. Jacobson. A celebrated figure among cruciverbalists, notably for her annual presence in the American Crossword Puzzle Tournament, she stayed with *New York* until 2011, contributing more than 1,400 puzzles before her retirement. Maura recommended a successor named Cathy Allis (formerly Cathy Millhauser), who had come to prominence with the *New York Times.* There, she once collaborated on the construction of a Sunday puzzle with former president Bill Clinton (a big crossword fan). Cathy quickly established that she was every bit the charmer on *New York*'s pages that Maura had been.

Do you need proof of that charm? In a puzzle she constructed for *New York* called "Getting Noshes," the clue "Physical affection with servings of Jewish derma?" led to the answer HUGS AND KISHKES. "Song during a wait for a Jewish deli treat?" SOMEDAY MY BLINTZ WILL COME. Her grids are notably full of clever theme clues, and her jokes are wry and playful but never forced. Even when making the "fill," the parts of the grid that are unthemed, she'll toss out a playful clue like "Ninths on diamonds," the answer to which is INNINGS.

What you've got in your hands is a collection of fifty of Cathy's puzzles, constructed over seven years. They're presented not quite chronologically but are arranged instead by month: That is, as you make your way through the book, you'll proceed from puzzles that appeared in January issues to those from December. (It doesn't include "Getting Noshes," so we haven't spoiled that one.)

As a bit of lagniappe, at the back of this volume we've included the first of those maddening puzzles constructed by Stephen Sondheim for *New York*'s early issues. If you're not used to cryptic crosswords, you may find it difficult; it requires that a double meaning be unpacked from each clue and then a theme applied atop that. (See our brief explanation on page 54.) The upside, of course, is the mental click that comes from figuring out something tough. Which, when you think about it, is a defining characteristic of New Yorkers themselves.

New York

CROSSWORDS

From *New York* Magazine...

Across

1 Billion: prefix
5 Like Kojak
9 Passport endorsements
14 Rustler-nabbing group
19 Hockey's Bobby et al.
20 Pulitzer-winning author Jennifer
21 In reserve
22 Flu symptoms
23 ...Snappy Comebacks Get Our Approval =
26 Brings up
27 Houston-to-Dallas dir.
28 Strings strummed in HI
29 Ken or Lena of film
30 Caterpillar, for one
31 Scrapes (out)
33 ...Soul Musical Overseer Hits the Right Notes =
38 Util.-bill component
40 San Francisco's —— Hill
41 Looks (at) angrily
42 Small armed ship
45 Vardalos and Long
47 Sounds at shearings
48 Hoopla
51 "Back ——!" ("Likewise!")
52 Male ducks
54 Confessional disclosures
55 Wardrobe woe
56 —— culpa
57 Couturier Christian
58 Tonic opener?
60 Show the ropes
63 Directional suffix
64 ...Munchkinland: I Came To =
69 Lover boy
71 Painter Cézanne
72 Footless animal
73 Bridal-shop buys
76 ...Fur Dyed for St. Paddy's Day? OMG! =
80 Nada
81 Songlike
83 Chinese Red Army leader
84 Menthol-cigarette brand
85 "Yo, Nero!"
86 "The New Yorker" cartoonist Chast
87 Off-color
90 Damon, creator of "Guys and Dolls" characters
93 Cry from a flock
94 Little "piggy"
95 Part of Saigon's current name
96 The Flintstones' pet
97 Downward course
99 Liberation
101 Mover on the Hill
103 Laura of "The Fault in Our Stars"
104 ...Keep At It, Madcap Vintner! =
109 Smutty
111 Looks —— everything
112 Grp. with crude interests?
113 Innocence-claiming phrase
115 Stomach-punch groan
117 Very, to Verdi
118 ...I Wore Sheer Fabric for the Whole Fashion Show =
122 Beneath
123 Thomas Jefferson, religiously
124 Lost a lap?
125 Timetable, briefly
126 Warty-skinned croakers
127 Tilts
128 Starting stake
129 Jekyll's counterpart

Down

1 Bridal-shop buy
2 Cara of "Fame"
3 ...You Can Do African Corn Farming! =
4 Inquire
5 Schnozz
6 Resigner before Nixon
7 Stocks up on
8 Subj. of a pop test?
9 "Presto!"
10 Ninths on diamonds
11 Indicate a turn
12 Many a Serena 17-Down
13 Rev.'s address
14 Sitting rooms
15 Antarctic and Atlantic
16 Predatory type
17 Tennis opening
18 Literature-class assignment
24 Madrid's —— del Prado
25 Horror-film staple
32 Actor Idris
34 Fall fast asleep (with "out")
35 Desert on the Silk Road
36 One who played Obi-Wan
37 Think logically
39 Southern Spanish province
42 PlayStation enthusiast, e.g.
43 In —— (prenatal)
44 —— l'oeil
46 Largest of a septet
48 ...Do Guys Who Live Near the Sphinx Seem Off? =
49 Relentless noise
50 Choose
53 Early Indo-European
54 Lather-covered
57 French ones take panes
59 Love-letter abbr.
61 Competitor
62 Suffix with serpent
65 Gin chaser?
66 Director Kazan
67 Eccentric
68 1994 Johnny Depp title role
70 Teamwork deterrent
74 Energize
75 Forked over
77 In a creepy way
78 Sushi seaweed
79 Divided into districts
81 Frick Collection collection
82 Milne marsupial
88 Once again
89 Tea, India-style
91 Empty out luggage
92 Alcove
93 Plot part
95 Wise guides
96 Most profound
98 Baseball commissioner Bud
99 Launched a tirade
100 Strand at a chalet, say
102 "Imagine" singer
104 Full range
105 University of Maine's home
106 F. Scott Fitzgerald's wife
107 Encounters
108 Henhouse perch
110 Slept lightly
114 Palm, e.g.
116 Grow dim
118 XL squared
119 Apt anagram of "aye"
120 SS supplement, maybe
121 Cookout residue

Do I Hear a W?

Across

1 Some plump-looking boots
5 Tissue-box word
8 Horace's "—— Poetica"
11 Soft shoe?
18 Tom Sawyer's aunt
20 Ornamental shoulder piece
22 Citrus drink
23 Heads-up from a worker glimpsing a couple of mice?
25 Clothing
26 How a stunt may be done
27 Playing "Jeopardy!" requires it
29 Billionth: prefix
30 W. Coast winter hrs.
31 Abs exercise
34 Charlie Chaplin's last wife
35 Asset
37 "Isn't room for us here, Mary. Better find a stable!"?
42 Greek H's
45 Variety
46 Coats from stoats
47 With 74-Down, a liqueur brand
48 "Time for you to be annoying again!"?
54 Hunch
56 Muesli relative
57 Fails to
60 Scrabble-tile holders
61 Mess up
62 Hindu causality concept
65 Vivacity
66 Biblical transport
67 Speaker's platform
69 What's pledged in a tomahawk-limitation treaty?
72 Hardly beastly
76 MDs who deliver
78 Jazz duet?
79 Escorted from outside
81 Pickup truck since 1981
82 Prince Harry, to little Prince George
85 Cold Italian treat
87 It may be "for the road"
89 Ontario's capital
91 Big problem for a broadcaster?
94 Doce months
95 Hinged metal fastener
97 Skosh
98 Cafeteria item
99 Query to a bag of soil missing its price tag?
107 Variety
108 "See ya, Signor!"
109 Decrease
110 Jackie O's second
113 Heyerdahl's Kon-Tiki, e.g.
115 Orderly piles
117 Made parallel
119 Cellulose —— (old base for film)
122 "I ain't buyin' that stomach-bug excuse!"?
125 Resin-based varnish
126 Not yet nabbed, maybe
127 Debussy contemporary Erik
128 Bears witness
129 Palindromic ABBA song
130 Card-game cry
131 PC alternatives

Down

1 On a ship's flying bridge, say
2 Graduation attire
3 Exult smugly
4 Malamute's load
5 Spanish coin, pre-euro
6 Hosp. caregiver
7 7 ft., 6 in. hoopster Ming
8 "Foreign Affairs" novelist Lurie
9 Suppose, informally
10 Biergarten vessels
11 Smelting residue
12 Guff
13 Little rascal
14 Bit of a Mr. Goodbar
15 Like ticks and heartworms
16 Site of an early fall?
17 Move, in Realtor-speak
19 It raises dough
21 Actress Hagen
24 Kardashian matriarch
28 Ingénue
32 Part of CPU
33 Tommy Lee Jones's sport
35 Untainted
36 Modern surgical tools
37 I.D. on a dust jacket
38 "—— you not" (Jack Paar catchphrase)
39 Hair or grass clump
40 Bay of pigs?
41 Badgers
42 —— on (goaded)
43 Latin land
44 Company that made Pong
49 Not snafu
50 Kilt-wearing kindred
51 Corn-syrup brand
52 Full-bodied: It.
53 "Felicity" star Russell
55 Endure
58 Flowerpot spot
59 Lymph ——
63 Puzzle involving pathways
64 Skater's jump
66 Mimicry
68 Sans a co-pilot
70 Pinto is one kind
71 Thick Japanese noodle
73 Like a loud crowd
74 See 47-Across
75 Manicurist's abrasive
77 1959 Heston film epic
80 Keep after taxes
82 Sundance Resort's state
83 Tot's taboo
84 Some facial wrinkles
85 "My stars!"
86 "Beetle Bailey" dog
88 It might eat your hat
90 Mediator's asset
92 Load of loot
93 Prefix with logical
96 Covenant
100 Mark with blotches
101 Vaqueros' ropes
102 —— his own
103 Rubes
104 Rouse
105 Depend (on)
106 Lady Antebellum and Rascal Flatts, e.g.
110 Author Brookner or Shreve
111 Dig find
112 Runs in neutral
113 Tabula ——
114 Number after sieben
115 Brief moments, briefly
116 Doo-wop syllable
118 American territory in the Pacific
120 Franken and Gore
121 Bit of bod ink
123 .0000001 joule
124 Hi-tech visual effects: abbr.

Wacky Weather

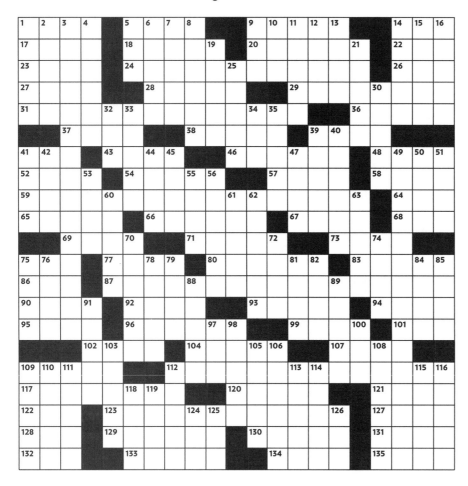

Across

1 Furry feet
5 Priestly vestments
9 Landfill filler
14 Samovar, e.g.
17 "Dies —" (requiem hymn)
18 Napped, say
20 "The Perfect Storm" (2000), et al.
22 — kwon do
23 Spirited tune
24 Parting words rephrased for frigid weather?
26 "Now — seen everything!"
27 Native of Riga or Liepaja
28 Hajji's destination
29 Went over, in a way
31 The Chiffons' song about a weatherman?
36 Bologna container?
37 Bring up
38 Get-go
39 Actress Remini
41 Pressure system affecting the weather
43 Any of the Bee Gees
46 Like some rye bread
48 "The Simpsons" bus driver
52 Fail to mention
54 Tedious to read
57 A bout place
58 "Pygmalion" playwright
59 Wearing a stormy-weather hat?
64 Program-file-name suffix
65 Inch stealthily
66 Tooth tissue
67 Novice
68 Give a hand
69 Give a hand?
71 Variety show
73 Deer sir?
75 "Well, yeah!"
77 Often-ticklish digits
80 Nobelist poet Pablo
83 Crosswise to a keel
86 Self-proclaimed psychic Geller
87 What happened in "stony" weather?
90 Cabbage variety
92 Footnote ditto, briefly
93 Kind of boom
94 "Snap out —!"
95 Jazz's Fitzgerald
96 Perpetrate
99 Hoity-toity sort
101 Scale notes
102 Whole lot
104 "Raining cats and dogs," e.g.
107 Archie Bunker creator Norman
109 Marisa of "The Lincoln Lawyer"
112 Nonchalant winter-weather report?
117 American-government personification
120 Situated at a junction
121 Fashion's Wang
122 Trip part
123 Latin-based saying about a storm that passes quickly?
127 Polo shirt brand
128 Take to court
129 Show the ropes
130 Blood's partner
131 Trigonometry ratio
132 Big galoot
133 Stocking color
134 It touted a "tiger in your tank"
135 Geraint's lady

Down

1 Edible tablets
2 Disney mermaid
3 Bygone gossip columnist turned weatherman?
4 Parlor piece
5 Shade of blond
6 Alpaca's cousin
7 Cut at an angle
8 Tiny bits
9 "OMG, enough details!"
10 Mythical big bird
11 Fern's brother in "Charlotte's Web"
12 Slaw or fries
13 Miami hoopsters
14 City east of Syracuse
15 "Boléro" composer
16 Indigent
19 Silently understood
21 Damascenes' homeland
25 Grannies
30 One of the Three Musketeers
32 Playground game
33 Hogwash
34 Test for advanced-deg. seekers
35 In — (prenatal)
39 Bruce posthumously pardoned by Pataki
40 Lawn-care tools
41 "The Family Guy" wife
42 Prefix with potent
44 Highlands hillside
45 Cap'n's mate
47 Power
49 Thomas Paine treatise disputin' global warmin'?
50 Airport limo alternative
51 Still had a bill
53 Charge at some crossings
55 Capital symbol
56 Aden citizen
60 Vaquero's lasso
61 Make merry
62 Promos on dust jackets
63 Complete
70 First responders, often
72 Multinational currency
74 "Peek- —!"
75 The Blue Devils from Durham
76 River to the Caspian
78 Nudge rudely
79 Leveling wedge
81 Crime bosses
82 Comparable
84 It covers a lot of ground
85 Citi Field team
88 Confess
89 Sometimes-dangerous bacterium
91 Stand in an art room
97 Passport, driver's lic., etc.
98 Quaint denial
100 Implore
103 Be dishonest with
105 Switch type
106 Separable component
108 Counsel
109 Oklahoma city
110 Outdo
111 Old-time radio's Fibber
112 Jacob K. Javits Center architect
113 W-2 figures
114 Ecstasy
115 Brand-name suffix with rice
116 Filled with cargo
118 Many a Bosnian
119 Gal pal, in Paris
124 Part of ESL
125 Sault — Marie
126 E'en if

Sounds Like a Woman

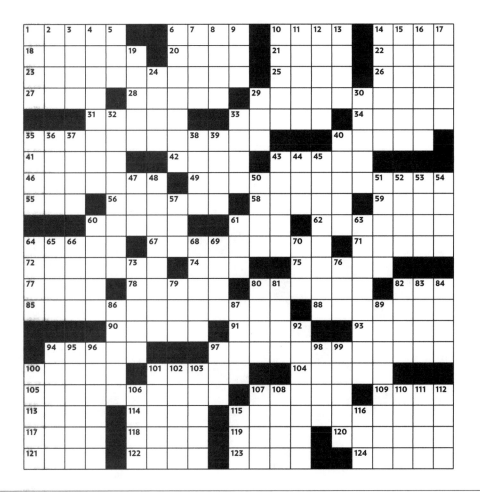

Across

1 Socially polished
6 French cleric
10 Identical
14 Coin-in-a-fountain thought
18 Dozing
20 Docent's duty
21 Fratricide victim in Genesis
22 Keen about
23 Period in which Lipinski held a figure-skating championship?
25 Southern-sounding sailboat
26 Boris Godunov, for one
27 Prado hangings
28 "I apologize"
29 With 35-Across, "That Tony-winning Rivera's never going to change"?
31 Octa-, halved
33 Steer clear of
34 Helpers
35 See 29-Across
40 Starting stakes
41 180 degrees from sur
42 Keyboarding flub
43 "Empire Falls" author Richard
46 Did what a pope first did on 12/12/12
49 Reason for actress Perlman to take Motrin?
55 Buddhist sect
56 Made level
58 Idolize
59 British peer above a viscount
60 Dove's desire
61 Band booking
62 Language of La Mancha
64 Great trait
67 Space-film character in the stratosphere?
71 Beehives and buns, e.g.
72 Source of comfort
74 ISP spun off Time Warner
75 "Saturday Night Live" segments
77 Pelvic bones
78 Mayor De Blasio's son
80 Rest of the group
82 Brazilian resort, for short
85 What Zeus may have done in pursuit of a Spartan queen?
88 Tries a phone number again
90 Beer first brewed in Brooklyn
91 Internet —— (viral phenomenon)
93 All, in stage directions
94 "Manhattan" director
97 "Mighty Aphrodite" star Sorvino, in profile?
100 Step in a flight
101 Appropriate as one's own
104 Absurd
105 Choose Miss Gabler, à la Ibsen's Mr. Tesman?
107 Micronesian nation in "Survivor" history
109 Frolic
113 Greek war god
114 Hodgepodge
115 "Vardalos has the final scene"?
117 Encircled
118 Not thound thober
119 Like Airedales' coats
120 Chooses for office
121 "Tiger in your tank" brand
122 Some tabbies and turkeys
123 Balm botanical
124 Playwright Clifford ("dotes" anagram)

Down

1 Fleetwood Mac title girl
2 Exploitative type
3 Touched down
4 Just loaf
5 Nightfall, poetically
6 Lure
7 Sow's mate
8 Lay to rest
9 Memorable past period
10 Anti-drug advice
11 Crude calculators
12 Spoke Manx?
13 Grammy-winning Fitzgerald
14 Hardly clueless
15 Like some jokes or jobs
16 Tabasco and Texas, e.g.
17 Bar mitzvah dances
19 Blog comments
24 "My kingdom —— horse!"
29 What aves lay
30 Paddled craft
32 Upper canines
33 Yours: Fr.
35 Bug-filled film of 1998
36 Rob of "Parks and Recreation"
37 Bird-named British architect
38 Overblown fanfare
39 Tablet debut of 2010
40 Embers, eventually
43 Mountain crest
44 Card game since 1971
45 Person barely running?
47 Mendes or Longoria
48 Festoon, say
50 Perform to a tee
51 Harvests
52 Flush, e.g.
53 Suffix with smack
54 Cure- —— (panaceas)
57 Pince- —— (old-style spectacles)
60 Floral corolla part
61 Hair goo
63 Disses
64 "In your dreams!"
65 Go it alone
66 Grub's habitat
68 "Maneater" singers Hall & ——
69 Advent song
70 Equivalent of -like
73 Meese, Moses, or Hubble
76 Indignation
79 Rangers' org.
80 Took too much, briefly
81 Domesticate
82 Sari-clad princess
83 A.J. Soprano portrayer Robert
84 Latin bones
86 Wagnerian work
87 Give off
89 Dunked
92 Sinister glance
94 Classic video-game systems
95 Magic and Kareem's team
96 Is dishonest with
97 Setting for pampering
98 —— uproar (tumultuous)
99 Lead-in to cologne or toilette
100 Phase
101 A Yo-Yo plays it
102 Intense hatred
103 Features of pheromones
106 Talk-show figure
107 Talk-show Dr.
108 Prefix with sol
110 Formerly
111 2012 loser to Barack
112 Skip a turn
115 It had a hub at JFK
116 Worldwide workers' grp.

Dual-Purpose Creatures

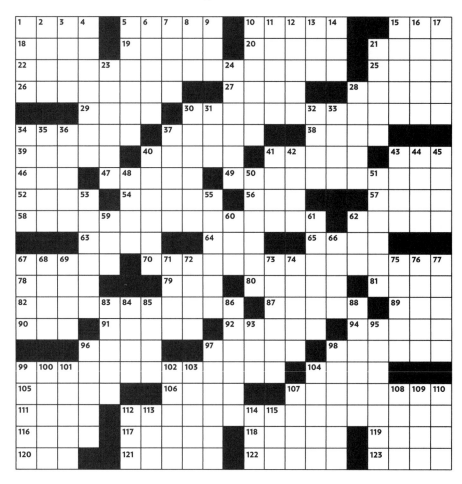

Across

1 ¿Cómo —— usted?
5 Unstressed-vowel symbol
10 Vaulted church recesses
15 Bout-enders at MSG
18 Gen- —— (post-boomer set)
19 "The Tempest" spirit
20 "Chicago Hope" Emmy winner Christine
21 Retained
22 Animal that might bark in the White House?
25 Brussels-based defense grp.
26 Insulted
27 Actress Naldi or Talbot
28 Part of SST
29 AAA suggestions
30 Produce a fleet-footed male animal?
34 "Ben-Hur" star
37 Physique
38 Membership payments
39 Top-tier invitees
40 "À —— santé!" ("To your health!")
41 Mexican father
43 Nintendo's Donkey Kong, e.g.
46 Diarist Anaïs
47 Family name at Tara
49 It would outshine a flea-circus performer?

52 Industrious sort
54 Cupcake component
56 Afore
57 Bona fide
58 Why the little parasite felt inferior?
62 Saunters, say
63 Commandment pronoun
64 Dallas NBA player, briefly
65 Turkey or fox chaser?
67 Teary-eyed
70 Result of a pet swallowing something it shouldn't?
78 Australia's national gemstone
79 Yoga-class need
80 Wrap that's not Glad
81 Foal's father
82 Do some male-animal poaching?
87 Ties up
89 110-Down, to a danseuse
90 Norton and Asner
91 Justice Sotomayor
92 Gush on stage
94 Number on a tag
96 Bindle-carrying drifter
97 John Williams composition
98 Gaps on forms
99 Why a vet might be called to the barnyard?
104 Table insert

105 Core group
106 Gambol
107 They turn bread brown
111 Hold sway
112 Manhandles an animal?
116 Egyptian fertility deity
117 Whoop it up
118 Comic-strip segment
119 Wander
120 Cotillion VIP
121 Kind of daisy
122 Chrysler Building topper
123 Scissors cut

Down

1 Montreal World's Fair, —— '67
2 Feudal worker
3 Nonkosher
4 States firmly
5 Turn blue?
6 First Nations group
7 Female red deer
8 Dewy
9 Frazier competitor
10 Banded together
11 Ristorante course
12 Bundle of wheat
13 Seventh Greek letter
14 Part of R.S.V.P.
15 Reeves of "Speed"
16 Vision-related

17 Market buy
21 Drawer hardware, maybe
23 Counting everything
24 Where harem pants are gathered
28 Dutch painter Jan
30 Genetic anomaly
31 Televise
32 Extra: abbr.
33 Daughter of ex-couple TomKat
34 —— Wipes (cleaning-cloth brand)
35 Poet who inspired "Cats"
36 Muscular strength
37 Yeltsin in Russian history
40 Appliance aimed at dust bunnies
41 Land of llamas and Lima
42 Fashion model Wek
43 Cain's victim
44 Acme
45 Slippery swimmers
48 Son: Sp.
50 It includes the hip bones
51 On the house
53 Fluster
55 Reproductive cell
59 Reticent
60 Wray of "King Kong"
61 Natural-gas component
62 Bowl-shaped frypan
66 Tear asunder
67 Speck
68 Tablet from Apple
69 Rival of Bloomie's and Barneys
71 Upscale hotel
72 Zilch, in Zaragoza
73 Jim who played Gomer Pyle
74 Old hat
75 Close-range hoops shot
76 Race place
77 Affirmative replies
83 In unison
84 Mongolian desert
85 Auth. unknown
86 Sums up
88 Bath-time sound
93 Perps' methods, for short
95 Roof supports
96 Root-beer brand
97 Mother of Dionysus
98 Fab Four member
99 Bitterly pungent
100 DVD-remote button
101 Improvise
102 Treasure stash
103 Corny
104 Hardly a social butterfly
107 Nobelist novelist Morrison
108 Black, to William Blake
109 Sitarist Shankar
110 Dance bit
112 —— -Magnon man
113 Whammy
114 Good periods
115 Mushy food

Medicine's a Business

Across

1 Egyptian Christians
6 Former British leader Tony
11 Apple desktop since 1998
15 Wound vestige
19 President Garfield's middle name
20 Blackmore's "—— Doone"
21 Beloved, in "Rigoletto"
22 Forearm bone
23 Hosp. area for closely watched tykes?
25 Dutch cheese similar to Gouda
26 State with "Field of Dreams" fields
27 Prepare for a printing press
28 Industry making horse pills, e.g.?
31 Cannot stand
34 Jam-pack
35 Storage compartment
36 Italian wine region
40 With 92-Across, dental biz name, à la a song by Boston?
42 Item in a scull operation
43 Necklace fastener
45 "Iliad" city
46 What dermatologists might dub their practice?
51 Podiatry office appellation?
54 Guy from hell
56 It contains a lot of Turkey
57 Unceasing
58 Metallic mix
59 Mare-to-be
60 James and Jones of jazz
62 Ordeal
63 Country of Maple Leafs and Flames
64 Canyon edge
67 Gastroenterology enterprise?
70 Some graduate degs.
71 Tooth covering
73 Duty lists
74 Apartments, London-style
76 Alma ——
77 Reds Hall of Famer Tony
78 Built
82 Golden Rule word
83 High points
84 Dietitian's office?
87 Chain of opticians?
89 Nickelodeon title explorer
90 Steakhouse order
91 Brewery tank
92 See 40-Across
96 Pronto, on a memo
97 Get
101 Battery fluid
102 "John B.," in a Beach Boys song
104 Endocrinology complex?
107 New York tribe
112 Yearn
113 Egyptian fertility deity
114 Obstetrics and gynecology provider?
117 Heart test readouts, for short
118 Collective defense org.
119 Mrs. Ralph Kramden
120 Eastern concept involving consequences
121 Breather
122 Composer —— Carlo Menotti
123 "Bullitt" Director Peter
124 Look of scorn

Down

1 Rank of Verne's Nemo: abbr.
2 Follow orders
3 Make ready, briefly
4 Steal
5 Huge hit
6 Not just tipsy
7 Privy, to Prince William
8 "Entourage" character Gold
9 Machu Picchu dweller
10 Lewd
11 Vendor who had a cool job?
12 No sir, she
13 Shrinking Asian sea
14 Gripe
15 "Poison" shrub
16 Singer Petula
17 Manga-like movie medium
18 Fuzzbuster's finding
24 Rafter, e.g.
29 401(k) kin
30 —— & Hardart (old automat company)
32 Art Deco luminary
33 Bone-dry
36 Unwelcome spots for teens?
37 Opening at an arcade
38 Domesticate
39 Grenoble's river (Eries anagram)
41 Preschooler
42 "Sure!"
44 Pink cartoon feline
46 Minn. coll. named for Norway's patron
47 Slayer of Abel
48 Faith observed in mosques
49 Oscar-winner Swinton
50 Rolling Stones album "Get Your —— Out"
52 Birth-related
53 Envelope part
54 Opens an envelope, maybe
55 Banned fruit pesticide
58 Desilu co-owner
59 Most fleet
61 Array inviting pig-outs
62 French heads
63 Barton or Bow
64 Uncle telling Br'er Rabbit tales
65 Absurd
66 Glossy alternative
68 Hershey brand —— Peppermint Pattie
69 Robert who played A.J. Soprano
72 "Feed this kitty!"
75 Acronymic diving gear
77 Bombard, à la hail
79 Madre's brothers
80 Active Sicilian volcano
81 Profound
83 Strutting like a spirited steed
84 Cambodian exile Lon ——
85 Addresses starting http://
86 A veterinary doc may dock it
88 "Metamorphoses" writer
89 —— with (eliminated)
92 Follows through with
93 Cedar relative
94 Gallows loops
95 Extinct
97 One leering lecherously
98 Chap
99 Shanks fitting into tool handles
100 Inner strife
101 "The Pilot's Wife" author Shreve
103 Extras for execs
105 Morales of "NYPD Blue"
106 "Copacabana" showgirl
108 Tennis champ Lendl
109 Gravely urgent
110 High point
111 Char
115 Sch. in Cambridge, Mass.
116 Pre-Christ: abbr.

9

The "More" the Merrier

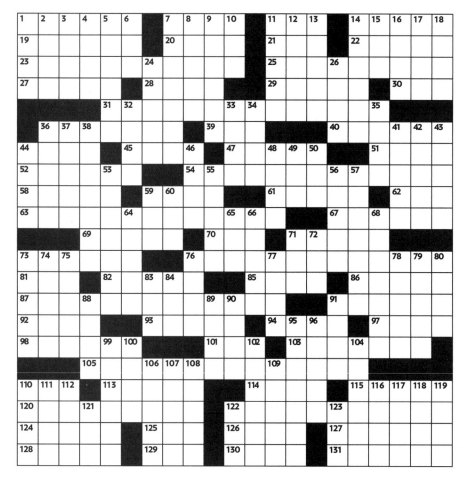

Across

1 Andy Warhol's genre
7 Pre-1917 ruler
11 Clock-setting std.
14 Cap Rembrandt wore
19 Expresses one's views
20 Other: Sp.
21 Organ with a drum
22 Hold forth
23 Slashed some durable pants?
25 Authentic southern dish?
27 Irish character actor Milo
28 Tennis's Nastase
29 Capital of Ghana
30 Aficionado
31 Conjecture about a full-fringe hairdo?
36 Public image
39 A caddy may hold it
40 Audio buy
44 Mont Blanc, par exemple
45 Toasty
47 Aquarium buildup
51 Succotash bean
52 __ d' (headwaiter)
54 Did an optician's job?
58 Looped handles
59 "Phooey!"
61 Twangy-sounding
62 Luau souvenir
63 Solidly packaged kids' dexterity game?
67 Stops
69 James and Jones of jazz
70 Conducted
71 "Religulous" satirist Bill
73 Seyfried who debuted in "Mean Girls"
76 Singer Bice's inner circle, as a young child?
81 Great Lakes' __ Canals
82 San Antonio landmark
85 Many a staffer
86 Avid
87 Cowboy's words on ditching some worn-out clothing?
91 Out-and-out
92 "¿Cómo __ usted?"
93 Offspring
94 "Wait just __!"
97 Forearm bone
98 Become misty-eyed
101 Jamaican music genre
103 Prioritizes, in emergency rooms
105 Near divers with decompression sickness?
110 Stooge with a bowl cut
113 "Who can that be?" response
114 Wander
115 Milne marsupial mom
120 In a field of plants that flavor beer?
122 Itchy condition affecting comedian Samantha?
124 Coat under varnish, often
125 Air safety grp.
126 Chief
127 Countercultural cartoonist Crumb
128 Flat-rental sign
129 Actor Mahershala of "Moonlight"
130 Carmaker of yore
131 Egg rating

Down

1 Somewhat, in scores
2 Numbered composition
3 Essence
4 Starting stake
5 Treatment sites for users
6 Prufrock poet's monogram
7 Useful row of icons
8 Narrow groove
9 Passionate
10 Coll.-dorm VIPs
11 Insinuate
12 Protest of a sort
13 Halt in hostilities
14 "The African Queen" co-star
15 Drop the ball
16 Game changer?
17 Ides rebuke
18 Try out
24 Aetna competitor
26 Lover of Psyche
32 "__ you one!"
33 Paraphernalia
34 Polio-vaccine developer
35 Sharp bark
36 Initial strategy
37 Anglican denom., here
38 Done over, as photos
41 Cambodian cash
42 Roast VIP
43 Camel caravan's stop
44 Key with three sharps: abbr.
46 Air-kiss sound
48 Boomers' kids, for short
49 Nabokov-title heroine
50 Greek goddess of dawn
53 Athlete's downtime
55 "SNL" alumna Cheri
56 Kind of chip
57 Unexpected hit
59 Crime-lab sample
60 Some NFL linemen
64 Novelist Calvino
65 It flies, or hits flies
66 Ready for use
68 Hallway runner, say
71 T-shirt-label abbr.
72 Prez on a five
73 Good point
74 Caribou's cousin
75 Vital heart vessel
76 Set of points
77 Simpsons kid voiced by Yeardley
78 Identical, to Yvette
79 Keystone State founder and family
80 Miss, in Mex.
83 S. Hawking lived with it
84 XL squared
88 Like an endangered avis
89 Multitude
90 Egyptian cross
91 Biting
95 Cat now named Yusuf Islam
96 White-tailed sea eagles
99 Pressing
100 "Hunny"-loving bear
102 From on high
104 Request
106 Home of the brave, briefly
107 Largely Hindu Himalayan land
108 Mother-daughter authors Anita and Kiran
109 Ox, goat, or sheep, e.g.
110 It's square-rigged on a brig
111 The "O" in FAO Schwarz
112 List-ending Lat.
116 "Dancing Queen" band
117 Indigence
118 "Pretty Woman" star Richard
119 "The Thin Man" dog
121 Hurry, quaintly
122 Med. provider group . . .
123 . . . and what one of its ltrs. means

Describe the Clues

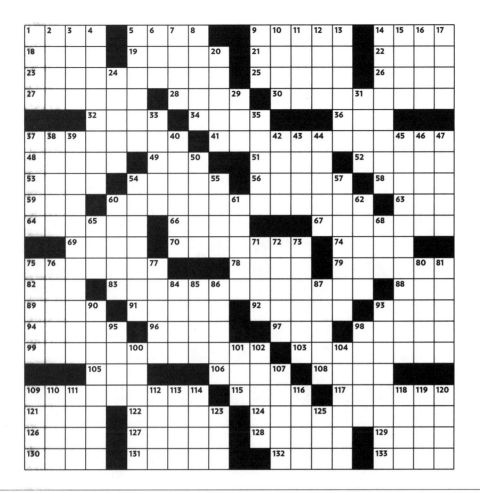

Across

1 Defraud
5 "Incredible" comics hero
9 Disconcert
14 Cat's "Scat!"
18 Her, in Le Havre
19 Spring Zodiac sign
21 Sporty former Toyota
22 Thumb-twiddling
23 *Manila?*
25 Former senator Lott
26 Tuckered out
27 Espionage
28 List-ending abbr.
30 *Bather?*
32 Purim's month
34 Procedure in assemblage
36 Suffix with racket
37 Traded a cow for a plow, e.g.
41 *Craned?*
48 Healing succulents
49 Lucy of "Kill Bill"
51 Kolkata dress
52 The D in LED
53 Droops
54 1988 film "A Fish Called ——"
56 Like week-old bread
58 "Move your bloomin' ——!" (Eliza Doolittle cry at Ascot)
59 Capote nickname
60 *Glibness?*
63 Sun.-sermon giver
64 Chef Lagasse
66 McEntire of country
67 In general
69 "The Bronx? No thonx" poet
70 Ancient seers
74 Branch of an Austin sch.
75 Bursts of light
78 Lighten
79 Had a flat?
82 Double-crosser
83 *Tastes?*
88 Home to St. Pete and Jax
89 Ring around a pupil
91 Certain distance runner
92 Far from flimsy
93 Calf-length skirt
94 Skirt
96 "Hairy" twin in Genesis
97 According to
98 Planetary extremes
99 *Maples?*
103 Industrial purification plant
105 Chapter of history
106 Powdery mineral
108 Early 007 film foe
109 *Dora?*
115 Noggin

117 De facto
121 Mine: Fr.
122 Incurred, as debts
124 *Shore?*
126 Cop fighting traffic?
127 Furry aquatic frolicker
128 Old Plains dwelling
129 D.C. ball team, briefly
130 Taxing hike
131 Like beluga whales
132 Look after
133 Yalies

Down

1 Hems or darns
2 YouTube bit
3 Treaty partner
4 Helps in arbitration
5 Plane site
6 "Psychic" Geller
7 Mojito fruit
8 "Ode to a Nightingale" poet
9 Well-chosen
10 Stinging remark
11 Out on the deep
12 Transmit
13 Hub of burgeoning activity
14 Classical name for Ireland
15 Notion
16 Crate or crib strip
17 Rogen of "The Interview"
20 List of candidates
24 Large portion of Chile
29 Ave. parallel to Mad. and Park
31 Take in the mail?
33 Kick back
35 Search party in oaters
37 Tend to a hem or a ham
38 Theft deterrent
39 *Anoint?*
40 Dough, to Hernando
42 Ink à la Popeye's anchors
43 Sr. income sources
44 Tiny hairs
45 *Life?*
46 Ill-fated fifties Ford
47 "Still Me" author Christopher
50 Calf's suckling site
54 The younger Grimm brother
55 Swedish singers of "SOS"
57 Made certain
60 Baryshnikov's nickname
61 Spiked
62 Microsoft co-founder
65 Coll.-dorm VIPs
68 TV cartoon Chihuahua
71 Bonny gal
72 Prevent legally
73 Paint base coat, e.g.
75 Mendicant-order member
76 Caterpillar or grub
77 Swine's confines
80 One with seniority
81 TV Duke or Duck
84 Disney's "Frozen" Snow Queen
85 Paper quantity
86 Have an outburst
87 Tuckered out
90 Robin, to Batman
93 Unvarying, dull voice
95 Small fishing boat
98 —— hitter
100 Bone-cavity tissue
101 Where sci. tests are hands-on
102 Choose
104 Tattered at the edges
107 Insertion symbol
109 Deliver a tirade
110 WWII's General Bradley
111 Central part
112 Inauguration highlight
113 Opposed to
114 Many a love song
116 Scruff
118 Eurasia's —— Mountains
119 Spumante region
120 Not so much
123 Opposite of post-
125 Sect stressing meditation

11

Oldies Remixes

Across

1 Starts the kitty
6 Play a banjo, perhaps
11 Gent's address for a lady
15 Be in a stew
19 "Queen of Mean" Helmsley
20 Sphere of activity
21 Bullets and BBs
22 Important caucus state
23 "Too Much Fabric" (Bob Dylan '75–Bobby Vinton '63)
27 Mel in Giants history
28 Hollywood's Gardner
29 Objective
30 Lays to rest
31 "I Want to See Our Old Photos" (Peter Frampton '75–Barbra Streisand '73)
37 Make public
38 Prefix with dermis
39 Tubular pasta
40 Combat-ready
44 Exuberance
47 Pained bark
49 Pester
51 Livy's "I love"
52 "I Ogled, Dear Psychiatrist" (Jackson Browne '72–Frankie Valli '74)
60 Actuarial datum
61 Passport endorsements
62 R&B singer —— James
63 Dolts
64 Chic, in the sixties
65 Pre-calc. math subj.
66 Subside, as rain
68 Ash, e.g.
69 "I Hope I'm the Father" (the Beatles '70–the Ronettes '63)
75 Many a Saudi
79 Chew out
80 Lingerie buy
81 Darling once with the Mets
84 Choose
87 "Beetle Bailey" dog
88 Polite refusal
90 Foreigner's "Cold As ——"
91 "Don't Let That Girl Cheat on the Diet" (the Zombies '64–the Guess Who '70)
95 A Gabor sister
96 Perrier, par exemple
97 Some hold Promise
98 Entwistle played it for the Who
99 Make a new A-line line
101 Carnaby Street district
105 Eton john
106 Grp. that runs the Loop's L
108 "Secure Those Shingles" (Archie Bell & the Drells '68–the Drifters '62)
115 City near San Diego
118 Dots in la mer
119 Break bread
120 CAT-scan alternative
121 "The Seven Dwarfs Seem Odd" (Randy Newman '77–the Doors '67)
127 Org.
128 Apart from this
129 "The Jetsons"'s Rosie, e.g.
130 Like some drones
131 Schlepping bag
132 Industrious sort
133 Nutritious potato parts
134 Tolerate

Down

1 Chorus section
2 Poetic "below"
3 Lone Ranger's sidekick
4 Part of ESL: abbr.
5 Italian sub meat
6 Co-Nobelist with Begin
7 Capote-themed play
8 VIP on the Hill
9 Prefix with lateral
10 Japanese comic-book genre
11 Africa's Nyasaland, now
12 Protective charm
13 Soul: Fr.
14 1968's "Yellow Submarine," e.g.
15 Coffee pod component
16 Wander
17 Washstand pitcher
18 Body art also called ink
24 Always
25 1991 film "—— n the Hood"
26 Fuming
32 Crave
33 Outkast hit of 2003
34 Modern pentathlon weapons
35 Skilled at scheming
36 Certain sot
41 Ed Koch memoir
42 Ham it up
43 Extinguish
44 Red-clad Dutch cheese
45 The Hartford's stag, e.g.
46 Breezed through
48 Burned rubber, in other slang
50 D-Backs, on scoreboards
53 Track shape
54 Vex
55 Some senior NCOs
56 Stern's opposite
57 ABA member
58 Smear (on)
59 Morse code character
67 "Blue Ribbon" beer
70 Symbol on a toolbar
71 Dorothy's dog
72 Sandwiches ordered alphabetically?
73 Verve
74 Knitting need
75 Daisylike flower
76 Superman portrayer Christopher
77 "The God" of Islam
78 —— canto (singing style)
81 Capital of Latvia
82 "Draft Dodger Rag" singer Phil
83 Seines and trawls
85 Linus Pauling was one
86 It's often in hot water
88 "The Phantom Menace" planet
89 Director Welles
92 Make tracks
93 Chug
94 Letter-shaped beam
100 Perpetual, to Shakespeare
102 Lazy
103 Assistant
104 First-year J.D. student
106 Shoot the breeze
107 Colorful aquarium fish
109 Stared openmouthed
110 Tech-support clients
111 Dry runs
112 Everything, to Virgil
113 Lung, for one
114 Diabolical sort
115 Exam for a future 57-Down
116 "Got it!," à la Mr. Moto
117 The majority
122 "Evil Woman" band, briefly
123 NASA thumbs-up
124 Stat for Maris or Mantle
125 Seeming eternity
126 Fitting

Fool's Paradise

Car-pun-try

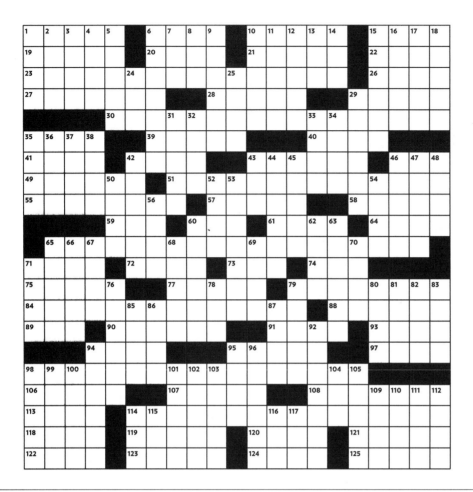

Across

1 High points
6 Buggy in Covent Garden
10 Mind's-eye view
15 ___ Crunch (Quaker brand)
19 Glow
20 Celebratory circle dance
21 Blood-drive participant
22 Miscellany
23 What a new car mechanic might be paid for?
26 Proposed law
27 New Testament letter
28 Harness race gaits
29 Morocco's capital
30 Car tunes, à la a Stevie Wonder album?
35 Hooved hybrid
39 Conan Doyle character Adler
40 Skip
41 Border on
42 Stage direction
43 Imp
46 Café-making need
49 Sell directly to consumers
51 Sight of a car in the desert, perhaps?
55 Shape on Turkey's flag
57 Ask (about)
58 Spring-blooming bulb
59 Author Umberto
60 "___ Wiedersehen"
61 Rick's "Casablanca" love
64 Knicks rivals
65 "Great coif to go with the car, huh?"?
71 Faris of TV's "Mom"
72 Just fair
73 H.S. math course
74 Sr. income source
75 Michelangelo statue in St. Peter's
77 Counting everything
79 Bratislava's country
84 Car belonging to Martini's partner?
88 Territory
89 It might move a mt.
90 "A Writer's Life" writer, Gay ___
91 Wife of Zeus
93 Kind of clef
94 Continental currency
95 Low-budget prefix
97 Horse-coat designation
98 Drama involving a car part, Alistair Cooke style?
106 Spam container, often
107 Husky with a Central Park statue
108 Horn & Hardart eatery, once
113 "Hold your horses!"
114 Sleuth who solves car problems, in a film spoof?
118 To be, to Bizet
119 Second showing
120 Agitate
121 New staffer
122 Went kaput
123 Health-insurance giant
124 Line of symmetry
125 Squash variety

Down

1 Queens-stadium surname
2 Dice
3 Marque of BMW
4 Rear-___ (strikes from behind)
5 Rears
6 Diamondbacks' city
7 Hold up
8 Knack
9 Aston ___ (many a James Bond car)
10 Blockhead
11 Nisan, for one
12 Ouzo flavoring
13 Suffix with poly
14 .0000001 joule
15 Blue shade or former Chevy
16 Suspect's story
17 Seasoned rice mixture
18 "Cape Fear" actor Nick
24 Half of ex-couple Bennifer
25 Duncan in Obama's cabinet
29 Rebuke harshly
31 Mill input
32 Bristle, in biology
33 Mayor before Dinkins
34 Apple debut of 1998
35 Fashion designer Jacobs
36 Prefix with mensch
37 Mandolin kin
38 Info on incoming flights
42 Votes in
43 "Self-Reliance" author's monogram
44 Being broadcast
45 Flair
46 Fished for congers
47 Samuel of the Supreme Court
48 Letter carriers' letters
50 "Law & Order: SVU" rapper turned actor
52 Color close to turquoise
53 Range-roaming herd of song
54 City-issued bond, briefly
56 Neighborhood w. of the Bowery
60 Does penance
62 Go by sloop
63 Dawn goddess
65 Negatively charged particle
66 Lifeless
67 D.C. ball team, for short
68 Parenthetical line
69 Societal troubles
70 Comedian Chappelle
71 Visit with a CPA, say
76 Real
78 Don't just seem
79 City near Florence
80 Food thickener
81 Part of kWh
82 Tiny amount
83 Soon, poetically
85 Instrument played by a Marx
86 "The Time Machine" race
87 Lead-in to horn or string
92 Pivots
94 Did a Salon job
95 Diminutive suffix
96 New Age guru Deepak ___
98 Cried like a kitten
99 Valuable violin
100 Congo's name, for a time
101 Colleague of Siskel and Roeper
102 Spicy Louisianian cuisine
103 Justice Kagan
104 McClanahan of "Maude"
105 ___ - Sketch (drawing toy)
109 Ear-related
110 Spanish surrealist Joan
111 Profess
112 Promgoer, typically
114 Song syllable
115 Half of a bray
116 Social reformer Dorothea
117 Ivy Leaguer nickname

Devilish Demonyms

Across

1 "Pygmalion" author's monogram
4 Soft mineral in powders
8 Completely wreck
13 Word with Nilla or Necco
19 Muesli grain
20 Territory
21 Love, Italian-style
22 Gives the slip
23 Possible nickname for a Nairobian hero?
26 Most stark
27 Fabled also-ran
28 Personal bearing
29 Infamous Amin
30 Tours of duty
31 Is mentally absorbed by a central South American?
36 Bout enders at MSG
37 Guzzle
38 Takes back, as a statement
42 Plane or file
44 HI strung instruments?
45 Oral history
46 Feline sign
47 Foresail
48 "Potemkin" mutiny port
51 R&B singer from a South Pacific island nation?
54 Schiller wrote one to Joy
55 Ventura County's —— Valley
56 Destines to failure
58 Devout
59 Audible response of horror
61 Small body-shop job
63 Skater Babilonia
64 Ship's front
66 Biblically "knowing" a native of Aden?
73 "The Fountainhead" author
74 Afore
75 Wet bar in a bathroom
76 Affirmative votes
77 "Li'l" guy from Dogpatch
80 Anne of "Archie Bunker's Place"
82 Tribe that fought Mormon settlers
84 Genetic-info carrier
85 Neil Simon's hotel-set story of a Nordic guest?
88 Landlord, in legal lingo
90 Hostel alternative
91 Fast asleep
92 Shipshape
93 Be philanthropic
94 "South Park" co-creator Parker
96 "The Tempest" magician
99 Compulsion
100 China's Long March leader
101 What happens when bosses fire just one from a Balkan land?
108 Do a security job
111 247.5 degs. on a compass
112 Revolutionary period?
113 Unspecified amount
114 Chao in George W.'s cabinet
115 Certain Southeast Asian getting bronzed?
118 Brass, in part
119 German appliance brand
120 Neuter, as male horses
121 Calendario square
122 Jousters' mounts
123 Actor Johnny and family
124 Husky's load
125 Big inits. in comedy skits

Down

1 Teens in black, perhaps
2 Faith founded in Persia
3 Opposite of 64-Across
4 Deck-swabbing gob
5 A Musketeer
6 Red Square honoree
7 The Citadel student, say
8 —— kwon do
9 Anthology of reprints
10 Shih Tzu or Yorkie, e.g.
11 Thin as ——
12 Writer Deighton
13 eBay, eHarmony, etc.
14 Personal icon online
15 Cooked wheat cereal
16 First place?
17 Sit a spell
18 Former fast fleet: abbr.
24 "Wall Street" role Gordon ——
25 Raps
32 They have bars for singles?
33 In first place
34 Pressing needs
35 Fashion's Wang
39 Lummox
40 Greenish-blue
41 PlayStation maker
42 Kind of basin or wave
43 Not just plump
44 On drugs
45 Boundaries
47 Runs for one's health
49 Bumped off
50 Make corrections to
51 2014 film starring Russell Crowe
52 Posthumous Pulitzer winner James
53 Tot's cry
57 Weasel-like swimmer
60 Rosie of "Fearless"
62 Like a coarse wool fabric
64 New York's Seneca County has two
65 Common blood-group designation
67 Prefix with trooper
68 "Dies ——" (requiem hymn)
69 Theater audience
70 Hauntingly strange
71 Her kids are animals
72 "No man —— island"
77 Each, informally
78 Unclear image
79 Intl. alliance acronym
80 A red Bordeaux
81 True up
83 Mlles., in Málaga
86 Ben Roethlisberger's team
87 Lean and muscular
89 Retailer Crabtree & ——
93 Adult
95 Avian perch
97 Indicator of rank
98 Rang up
99 Open with a click
100 Team or individual spirit
102 Cognizant
103 Safecrackers
104 Superman, on Krypton
105 Nullifies
106 At full throttle
107 Kidney-related
108 Muscles above abs
109 Scads
110 Watergate "smoking gun"
115 Abbr. meaning "not yet settled"
116 Bus. of Allstate or Aflac
117 Quirky

Literary Mash-ups

Across

1 Do a checkout task
5 Warmed the bench
8 Earring style
12 Investment firm Charles ——
18 Vaulter's need
19 Shade of color
20 Concise
21 Mrs. —— of Chicago Fire lore
22 "Sleeve" (E. M. Forster/Ernest Hemingway)?
25 Thrusting sword
26 Future and past perfect
27 Gardener, at times
28 None of the above
30 Smidgen
31 Away from port
33 Desert havens
35 Prefix with center
37 "Source of Wine-Fueled Jollity" (John Steinbeck/Edith Wharton)?
43 Teri's "Young Frankenstein" role
46 Roof overhang
47 Cornerstone abbr.
48 Battleship letters
49 Depicted, as with an MRI
51 Deep-red
54 UFO crew
56 Failed to tip
57 The Cards, on scorecards
58 "Animal Atop Thread" (Tennessee Williams/George Eliot)?
63 Malt suffix . . .
64 . . . and its meaning
66 Miller —— beer
67 See 59-Down
68 Bushed
70 Wilco guitarist Cline (lens anagram)
71 "Were you born ——?"
73 Beginner
74 Ibsen's "—— Gabler"
76 Egg: prefix
77 "Yo!," on a bus. env.
78 October birthstones
80 "Wheel of Fortune" buy
81 "Ladies Hit Some Booze" (D.H. Lawrence/J.D. Salinger)?
85 Agnus —— (Lamb of God)
87 Jones or Johnson, e.g.
89 Reagan's "Star Wars" plan: abbr.
90 Took as a given
92 Taco-products brand
93 Granola grain
95 Hold up
98 Ancient Persian
99 Brand of fruity sodas
100 "Fur Meets Jewelry in Manhattan" (John Updike/Truman Capote)?
105 North Pole worker
107 Finish second
108 Like a loud crowd
109 Flamenco cry
111 Phishing medium
113 "A Doll's House" protagonist
115 Often-itchy outbreaks
120 Pertain
122 "Tia and I: Swept Away" (Margaret Mitchell/Graham Greene)?
125 Part of BMOC
126 Online reminder
127 Its cap. is Abu Dhabi
128 "M*A*S*H" star
129 Evaluate
130 Embroiders, e.g.
131 Early Pink Floyd member Barrett
132 Complete flop

Down

1 Quarrel
2 Meet life's demands
3 Arkin of "Argo"
4 The Untouchables' leader
5 Daisy variety
6 Summer mo.
7 Giggling sounds
8 Learn secondhand
9 Hockey legend Bobby
10 Gradual-learning method
11 Harasses
12 Achy
13 Writer —— Booth Luce
14 With it, once
15 "Geezers Take So Long" (Samuel Beckett/Cormac McCarthy)?
16 Vicinity
17 Polar explorer Richard
20 Pointe dancer's pivot
23 Char
24 Best man's offering
29 F.D.R.'s successor
32 Bushed
34 Keep entertained
36 Singer Édith
37 Private eyes, slangily
38 Male red deer
39 "Bad Roots" (Agatha Christie/Eugene O'Neill)?
40 Jewel
41 Activist folk singer from Alabama
42 Chart toppers
44 V-formation flock
45 Threw in
50 Errs in texting
52 Rascal
53 Crew "sticks"
55 "Music From Big Pink" group
56 Fa follower
59 With 67-Across, Popeye's love
60 Sturdy sheer fabric
61 Onward
62 Mrs. Dick Cheney
65 Exam for H.S. dropouts
69 "Rosemary's Baby" author Levin
72 No hon, this Hun
73 Buzz Lightyear et al.
74 Is wearing
75 Accustom
76 Abode, Cockney-style
79 Far from posh
82 Epps or Sharif
83 Fatal suffix
84 Track odds, e.g.
86 Middle March
88 Astronaut Armstrong
91 Hollywood's Thurman
93 Does a favor for
94 Mother-of-pearl source
96 Video-game pioneer
97 Low-hanging cloud
101 Shrinks' org.
102 Doctrines
103 Raised cane?
104 Unravel from wear
106 Baby to be
109 "Free Willy"'s Willy, e.g.
110 Pastures
112 Neatnik's nightmare
114 Have debts
116 It made the car model 9-5
117 Streaming-video website
118 Wraps up
119 Sportscast fig.
121 O'Neill play, "The Hairy ——"
123 This instant
124 Pitchfork target

Prefix Mix-ups

Across

1 Language of Iran
6 Demolish
10 Legally invalid
14 Urban haze
18 A way to read
19 Midterm or final
20 Makeup magnate Lauder
22 Mob boss
23 Not mugging for the camera while directing surgery?
26 See 5-Down
27 Kuwaiti ruler
28 Coffeehouse vessels
29 "The Raven" poet's inits.
30 Twin, to his or her twin
32 "By the power vested ___ …"
34 Archipelago part
35 Crows' homes
36 Work of offing jailbirds?
43 Wind ensemble members
44 Torah cabinets
45 Fitness-regimen component
50 Trading places?
51 Foyer
53 Brewer's grain
55 Wine grape
56 Apt name for a cook?
57 Sage, for one
58 City of northern France
59 Finned mammalian killer
60 Fan out arranged all wrong, as a bungling marching band?
66 Goof up
67 Western flick
68 Noteworthy period
69 Slam legal phrases about staying open?
78 The Bard's river
79 The fable guy?
80 Position of control
81 Designated-driver alternative
83 Super 8, say
85 Nothing, in Nantes
86 Showy spring bloomer
88 Gillian Flynn best seller "___ Girl"
89 Diplomatic etiquette
91 Uplifting lingerie
92 United competitor
93 Person in favor of weight loss, say?
98 Say "say say", say
102 Longtime Yankees nickname
103 Licorice-flavored liqueur, in France
104 First name in a Beatles title
106 ATM-keypad input
107 Prefix with cultural
109 Corn Belt state
113 Takes to court
114 Sense one's former spouse is being too well taken care of?
118 Loafing
119 Grows dim
120 Like Airedales' coats
121 Salt away
122 Late finish?
123 Blog entry
124 Perform to a tee
125 Sophia of "Nine" (2009)

Down

1 Charge for 81-Across
2 Coll. endowment source
3 Rice-A- ___
4 Dawns
5 With 26-Across, infamous Ugandan despot
6 Rue
7 Neuron appendage
8 Nukes in the microwave
9 Ostrich's fast-running cousin
10 Kathmandu native
11 Final tennis Grand Slam event
12 Columbo and Kojak: abbr.
13 Dregs
14 It shows between cornrows
15 1950s First Lady
16 Speak one's mind
17 Music discs?
21 Person who rights copy
24 Deaden
25 Crows' homes
31 Forties jazz style
33 Greek consonants
34 Eww-inspiring
36 The po-po
37 The late news, in brief?
38 Still in bed
39 Maimonides was one
40 Wall St. maven, for short
41 Vintner Ernest or Julio
42 Yankees giant Derek
46 Ecological groupings by region
47 Letters on some crosses
48 Gabrielle Chanel, by nickname
49 Satirist Freberg (R.I.P.)
51 Find out
52 Chicago airport code
53 Tightwad
54 Actress Woodard
57 Horizontal kin of a Dagwood
58 All aglow
61 Cheesemaking substance
62 The rope of one's end?
63 Stoneworker
64 Like an old apple
65 Calla-lily family
69 Humid
70 Singer-actor Novello
71 Explorer Hernando de ___
72 Ricochet
73 Heroine in Bizet's "The Pearl Fishers" ("I, Ella" anagram)
74 Settled on
75 Spy novelist Deighton
76 Potentially dangerous bacterium
77 Domingo or Tomás
82 Noggin
84 Lindsay of "Mean Girls"
86 Goad
87 Musical aptitude
88 Starts relishing
90 Interrupt abruptly
91 Co-op City's borough
92 Early seventh-century year
94 Italian port noted for pizza
95 Professional in a confessional
96 Baseball's Strawberry
97 Course-work segment
98 Varnish ingredient
99 Slip away from
100 Facial treatments
101 Mitigates
105 Gather in
107 Athletic-shoe brand
108 Former Spice Girl Halliwell
110 Effect of halitosis
111 Used to be
112 Yemeni port
115 Old name for Tokyo
116 Part of BYOB
117 Subj. for new citizens

Product Placement

29 Dive like an eagle
32 Soprano Te Kanawa
33 Reacted to heartbreak
34 Stand up to
35 Miscellany
36 Pusher's customer
37 Swindles
38 Utters, slangily
39 Verdant foliage
42 Slot for a floppy disk
43 Day, at the Louvre
44 Calculating viper?
45 Great, on some diplomas
46 "Bi-winning" coiner Charlie
48 Breadth
50 Proficient
51 Seriously stout
54 What "a" or "I" may mean
55 Crack, as a code
59 Prefix with porosis
60 Gets the shampoo out
61 Bullring "Bravo!"
62 R.L. who created "Goosebumps"
63 Packs tightly
64 Embarkation station
65 Give goosebumps, maybe
67 Mighty long time
68 22.5 deg. compass point
71 Rapper/actor in "New Jack City"
74 Bowler's bedposts or Cincinnati
76 Take —— for the worse
79 Hacienda room
80 Flowerpot spot
81 Taxing journey
83 '60s sitcom set at Fort Courage
84 Fend off
85 Ferret's cousin
86 Suffix with Brooklyn
88 Figurative hiding places
92 Shredding
93 Where products are promoted in mags
95 Did a bagel-cooking step
96 Chinese dumpling
97 PC troubleshooter
98 Lifts with effort
99 Cat-story author Cleveland ——
100 Castor bean toxin used in poisonings
101 Student of Socrates
102 Thrust and parry
105 Life-or-death
106 Verve
107 Month before Nisan
108 Product of glacial calving
109 Umpire's call
111 Tree popular with squirrels
112 PB & J alternative
113 Post-op locale

Across

1 Foot in some poems
5 Like the Nissan Cube
9 Killer marine mammal
13 Squash is one
18 The Hudson River's "Clearwater," e.g.
20 Incantation start
21 Pile of loot
22 Drew on TV
23 Meat entrée
25 Much grapevine chatter
27 Granola grain
28 Openly condemn
29 Flue residue
30 Chant
31 Receding Asian sea
32 Skating champ Michelle
33 Wash
34 Effect of inebriation
39 Tests for Ph.D. hopefuls
40 Borden's mooing mascot
41 January, in Juarez
42 Met solo
43 Printer hassles
47 Pastures
49 1947 Oscar-winning Disney song
52 CUNY college in Queens
53 Hyannis's cape
56 Engendered
57 Yield just a bit

58 The —— State (Oklahoma)
61 "Havana" actress Lena
62 Utterly calm
63 LP successors
66 Fund-raisers, reunions, etc.
69 Wasn't colorfast
70 Reel off
72 "Picnic" playwright William
73 Baseball's Banks and golf's Els
75 Swiftly
76 Semicircular sanctuary area
77 Hokkaido dough
78 Sibilant "Ahem!"
82 Reason for leadership change
87 Cream-filled pastry
89 Don't dele
90 Mardi Gras day: abbr.
91 Scenic overlook sight
94 Northern French city
95 Utterance through chattering teeth
96 "Let's have a conversation"
98 Whaling weapon
102 Y branch?
103 Big galoots
104 Estevez, brother of 46-Down
105 Bit of progress
106 { or }
107 Six-pack muscles
110 Center of interest
112 What a lightbulb may symbolize

114 Hackneyed
115 With the bow, in music scores
116 The conga is done in it
117 Babushka
118 Church council
119 Incisive
120 Glad rags
121 Strong impulse

Down

1 A colon, in analogies
2 Jessica of "Sin City"
3 Not worth debating
4 Rock's —— Jovi
5 Hideout under Wayne Manor
6 Midwest college noted for early diversity
7 Picture of health?
8 Shaggy bovine Tibetan
9 Akron or Dayton native
10 Hazardous household gas
11 Group of zealots
12 Stout alternative
13 Treats with tea
14 Dish heavy in carbs
15 Bean once on Broadway
16 Tack straps
17 Melville's first novel
19 Did some spinning
24 Parched
26 Balm of —— (Biblical-named salve)

First World Problems

Across

1 French cleric
5 Taxing journey
9 Friends, in Firenze
14 Whacks
19 Parade spoiler
20 Wonderland tea-party animal
21 Wheels rented for proms
22 Nunnery toggery
23 "Oh no! My power went out and I can't ——"
26 2008 Person of the Year for 17-Down
27 Common jam fruits
28 "Gasp! I'm out of Aquafina; I'll have to drink ——"
30 Positive trait
31 Hecklers' sounds
32 Loch of legend
33 Radon or radium, e.g.
36 Bearlike bamboo muncher
39 Laurie of "House"
43 Not quite right
46 Metal in magnetite
47 Tibetan Buddhist teachers
48 Prefix with pod
49 "Horrors! The autoflush didn't work, so I had to ——"
53 Chinese noodle dish
56 Tells
57 Stow cargo
58 Extended skyward (over)
59 Sharp bark
60 "The outrage! This church ——"
63 Sirius medium
66 Seeped
67 "Poor me! My power came back on; now I have to ——"
74 Site of Napoleon's exile
78 Goes the Wright way?
79 Top-notch
80 Fear or loathing, say
83 Pointed retort
84 "Sob! These pants are too tight ——"
87 Break bread
88 Forties jazz style
89 Realty measure
90 As we speak
91 Haughty sort
93 WWII hero Murphy
94 Some Honshu natives
97 No beaut, this fruit
99 Shock jock Don
100 Retort to "You are not!"
104 "OMG! I bit into my chocolate-chip cookie, and it was ——"
110 Hide
112 San Antonio mission
113 "Sigh! My new Porsche is too low for the ——"
115 Gave a pink slip
116 Beneath
117 Jane Fonda, to Bridget
118 Suffix with smack
119 Gawk
120 Out of style
121 Golf-ball props
122 Stocking shades

Down

1 Resort site off Venezuela
2 Bags on a diamond
3 Stands holding coffins
4 Dinner-menu option
5 Quaker pronoun
6 "Curses!"
7 Mess up
8 Continue
9 Father-son actors Robert and Alan
10 Rosario's role in "Rent"
11 "Sign me up!"
12 Stallion-to-be
13 Roosevelt, Governors, and Ellis
14 Is evident
15 "The —— Cannonball"
16 Blind as ——
17 News magazine since 1923
18 Sirius, e.g.
24 Roster for a hired gun
25 Tons
29 Potpie morsel
31 Well: It.
34 Art Deco illustrator
35 Hardness-scale creator
36 Eucharist plate
37 Latin lover's verb
38 Tandoor-baked bread
40 Wombs
41 Bereavement reaction
42 Language of India
43 Nashville institution, familiarly
44 Gratis
45 Took a nosedive
47 Old Ford models
50 Maple-syrup source
51 Burst into flower
52 Oil-rich Mideast fed.
53 Nothing, to Rafael Nadal
54 Had a bill, still
55 Kitten's cry
58 "Looney Tunes" "devil", briefly
60 Cinco de Mayo, e.g.
61 Lugged
62 Carpooler's kind of lane, briefly
63 Repetitive learning method
64 Golden —— (senior citizen)
65 OBs and ENTs
67 Bulldozes
68 Perrier alternative
69 Mottled horse
70 Scott Joplin piece
71 Sierra Nevada lake
72 Ring around a barrel
73 Photo blowup: abbr.
74 Biblical verb ending
75 Narnia's Aslan, e.g.
76 U2 front man
77 Fresh way to start
80 Flemish painter Jan van ——
81 Actress Sorvino
82 Aperture
84 CNN founder Turner
85 —— -Wan Kenobi
86 Goats' bleats
88 Gradual accumulation
92 Real hassle
93 In the style of
94 Fail to mention
95 Beachgoer's bonnet
96 Scented pouch
98 Crystal-lined rock
99 Rhône tributary (Eries anagram)
101 Ben Stiller's mom, Anne
102 Squelched
103 "Stand and Deliver" actor Edward James ——
104 Clods
105 Landed
106 O'Hara plantation
107 Cellular component of protein synthesis: abbr.
108 Helps out
109 Lithographers Currier and ——
110 Scoop holder
111 Means of escape
114 Wish undone

Stuffed!

Across

1 Supports for injured arms
7 "Like, no way!"
11 Angry Birds, e.g.
14 Car-impoundment tasks
18 Jubilance
19 __ Ration (former dog food)
20 Links standard
21 Neglect to mention
22 "All Time High" ("Octopussy" theme) singer
24 Stephen of "The Crying Game"
25 Justice Sotomayor's alma mater
26 Astaire who danced in skirts
27 Pre-release version
28 Blunt in films
30 Formerly
31 Form of discrimination
33 Research component
36 The whole enchilada
38 Cut off
39 Purview
40 It may be manicured
43 PA-syst. part
45 Wannabe's model
47 Madrigal group, maybe
51 Menu phrase
52 Japanese floor mats
55 Bagel topper
58 Cincinnati's river
59 Part of MGM
61 Jazzman Kenton or Getz
62 Star in Orion
63 Landlord's income
64 Anatomical ring
66 50 Cent hit remix with Mobb Deep
69 Fruity frozen desserts
71 Hebrew name meaning "lion"
72 Figure-skating jump
75 "Quiet!", rudely
80 Military gesture
81 Grammy-winning Redding
83 Kashmir coin
84 Temporal brinks
86 Swiss host city of the World Economic Forum
87 Enthralled
88 Apple debut of 1998
89 Topics for Freud and Jung
91 DVR button
92 Ciabatta or chapati
94 FDR hometown __ Park
96 Shack
97 He loved Lucy
98 "¿__ está usted?"
101 Pinkish-orange
104 "Dies __" (requiem hymn)
106 South American capital
111 Legally bars
115 Ample, informally
116 Put off
117 Letters on invitations
119 Frame job
120 Boating hazard
121 1980s sitcom alien
122 Comedian Yakov Smirnoff's catchphrase about America
125 Use beams surgically
126 "Calvin and Hobbes" bully
127 Right-hand person
128 Makes swapping deals
129 Otherwise
130 Bit of flight-board info
131 Belgian river in WWI history
132 Takes the rudder

Down

1 Skid, e.g.
2 Allergen in some gloves
3 From Umbria
4 Most kindly
5 Slimy stuff
6 Hoity-toity type
7 Dogs of a Japanese breed
8 Staid
9 Gerund ender
10 Conned out of cash
11 Patriots' Day month
12 Spanish one-dish meal
13 Grace, say
14 Car still in production after 50 years
15 Muscat native
16 Ham's "Gotcha, I'm on it"
17 Dutch painter Jan
18 Historic stretches
23 Trailblazed
29 Downright dopey
32 NYC home of "The Starry Night"
34 Hertz rival
35 Corp. VIP
37 Comic strip named for a teen woe
40 Holy Tibetans
41 Last Oldsmobile produced
42 Hookah, e.g.
44 Roman censor whose name anagrams to what's found 8 times in the puzzle
46 Nike's Swoosh, for one
48 Paris landmark with a Pyramid
49 Austrian article
50 Rugrat
52 Available for a flat rate?
53 Egyptian __ (cat breed)
54 Amount consumed
56 Let off steam
57 Chorale section
60 High-caffeine product of a hardy plant
62 Ella of "Phantom Lady"
65 Arcade-game pioneer
67 Prefix with pod
68 Checks one's texts
70 Pond gunk
73 Plains tribe members
74 "My Cousin Vinny" star Joe
76 Fish whose name is a letter short of Winfrey's
77 Do an ecofriendly deed
78 Greens on Brown buildings
79 PC troubleshooter
81 Celestial body
82 Swabbie
85 Feng __ (Chinese practice)
89 Do meant to last
90 To be, to Bizet
93 The point of it?
95 Entrance with jambs
97 Thaw of a sort
99 Tussaud title
100 Leopardlike cat
102 Scrape away
103 Surgeon for whom a mouthwash is named
105 Give one's word to
106 "Uncle Miltie" of early TV
107 Tatum or Ryan
108 Shot in the dark
109 Rubbed out
110 "Selma" director DuVernay
112 Furry, web-footed swimmer
113 Sounds fine, as a feline
114 1974 CIA film spoof
118 Banned pollutants, briefly
123 __ Holiness, Pope Francis
124 Feedbag tidbit

Have ING Fun

Across

1 Meager
5 Garçon's handout
10 Classic comic-strip possum
14 At liberty
18 Prefix with sphere
19 Font akin to Helvetica
20 Wolfish look
21 Travels on a barque
22 Grateful words on actress Tate or Stone's birth?
25 Book in which the world is flat?
26 South Carolina river
27 Lacking slack
28 Really dirty
30 Within easy reach
31 Wrestler's goal
33 Give a detailed talk on a Mozart contemporary?
36 Reacted to a bad pun
39 I, to Claudius
40 D.C. ballplayer, briefly
41 Kimono, say
44 Chum at the nuclear-power plant?
47 "Popeye" Doyle, e.g.
50 Latin conjugation word
51 Pats down
52 Lawyer's "thing"
53 "Finding Nemo" female
54 Co. name ender
55 __ off (miffed)
56 American saint Elizabeth Ann
59 Allude (to)
60 Feline on the witness stand?
64 Chocolate treat named for a fungus
66 Women called bhikkhunis, in Buddhism
67 Circular edge
68 Agt.
70 Yours, in Tours
71 Sled dogs
74 Bring (someone) a mosslike organism?
79 Winds in the pit
80 Forte's opposite
82 Bulldog backers
83 "Family Guy" network
84 Pharma output
85 Body of eau
86 Pamper to excess
89 Ceremony of passage
90 Pitching stat
91 Result of making some calls from the Coliseum, e.g.?
94 Rival of Harrow
95 "Sprechen __ Deutsch?"
96 2013 Joaquin Phoenix film
97 Celebrations, in Santiago
99 Deemed indecent?
104 NY summer hrs.
105 Low-light retinal receptors
108 Hinders
109 Collectible caps in a 1990s fad
111 It gets smashed at parties
113 Pertaining to birth
114 Miracle fruit in the Gospel of John?
119 Cave under performance pressure
120 Sandy shade
121 Hearing-related
122 Ocean motion
123 Fritz Katzenjammer's twin
124 Profound
125 Roof options for some 'Vettes
126 "Orinoco Flow" singer

Down

1 Stays idle
2 Lindsay of "Freaky Friday"
3 Absurd
4 "In Memoriam" video tributes, often
5 Job for Columbo
6 Hound sound
7 Orinoco, por ejemplo
8 Granny Smith quality
9 Idina's "Frozen" character
10 Oliver Stone title army unit
11 Opposite of 'neath
12 It made Prizms
13 "Believe it __, …"
14 Rich big-shot
15 Poet James Whitcomb __
16 Spiral-horned antelope
17 German industrial city
21 Glide showily
23 "Galloping Gourmet" Graham
24 Arm-y greeting
29 Forms an attachment
31 Like chromosomes
32 Person with privileged knowledge
34 Bach's "Mass __ Minor"
35 Prefix with transmitter
37 Infraction
38 Hägar creator Browne
41 Commuting option
42 Hyatt alternative
43 Drink that goes with a "heart-attack snack"?
45 Peak in Greek myth
46 Bit of progress
47 You might have this at the undertaker's?
48 Baseball's Hershiser
49 Combustible heap
53 "Robinson Crusoe" author
55 North African capital
57 To be, to Henri
58 "Take __ Train"
59 Buzzi and Ginsburg
61 Microwaves, slangily
62 "Lovely" Beatles girl
63 Arabian Peninsula sultanate
65 Most risqué
69 Promised to give
71 Last word of "The Wizard of Oz"
72 Ridesourcing company
73 Email nuisance
75 Multibillionaire __ brothers
76 Least well
77 "Africa" band
78 Bovine plow pullers
81 Corporate raider Carl
85 Lerner's "Camelot" collaborator
87 Big galoot
88 Recovers from a drenching
89 Strike a chord
91 Enigma
92 After-tax amount
93 Arises
95 Furtive types
98 Nev. neighbor
99 Fictional lawyer Atticus
100 Warren Buffett's city
101 "The Jungle" author Sinclair
102 Comparable to a beet
103 "There is __ in team"
106 "Splish Splash" singer Bobby
107 Room in Clue
110 Tiny winged pest
111 Cronies
112 Out of port
115 Get a 100 on
116 Fury
117 To's partner
118 Race circuit

Likely Excuses

Across

1 Comic strip Brit Andy
5 Pleasingly shining
10 Lieu
15 Did laps, perhaps
19 Cookie in "dirt" pudding
20 Silents actress Bow
21 Pause mark
22 Constructed
23 "Assault? But the coach *told* us to —"
26 Pelvic bones
27 Low-ranging woodwinds
28 Sly look
29 Of yore
30 Stylish, in the '60s
31 "Murder? But the marriage counselor *told* me to —"
35 "Cheers" role for Rhea
39 Degraded
41 Lummoxes
42 WWII German fleet
44 Stretchy-bandage brand
45 — fatale
47 Person with a beat
50 "Defamation? But the teacher *told* me to —"
54 Homage in verse
55 Stick around
56 Afflicts
57 Gabbed nonstop
58 Coagulate
59 Barista's order
61 Not Rx
62 Dawn goddess
64 "Child endangerment? But the baby's dad *told* me to —"
70 Validates as fact
71 Edible stick slice
72 Cosmetician Lauder
73 Gin and tonic garnish
74 "Rugrats" girl
76 Jai — (court sport)
77 In addition
81 Egg cells
82 "Workplace aggression? But the boss *told* me to —"
86 Room for unwinding
87 Pile up
88 — Maria (coffee liqueur)
89 Given a napped leather finish
90 Jacob — Park, Queens
91 Overly proper
94 Fairway growth
95 "Deceit? But the shrink *told* me to —"
100 WWII command area
102 Rand McNally reference
103 Red-ink figure
104 Road edges
109 Go by
110 "Theft? But the liquor store owners *told* us to —"
114 Narrow cut
115 Author Desai or Bruckner
116 Privileged few
117 Tandoor, e.g.
118 Peacock feather features
119 Trite
120 Tons of, slangily
121 Capone's nemesis

Down

1 Tigers great Ty
2 Kind of code
3 Stew veggies
4 Cookware for stews
5 Sound before a blessing
6 Oscar Best Actress Jackson
7 Thailand neighbor
8 Table scrap
9 Baby's cry
10 Diatribe
11 Kind of pole on a reservation
12 Board used on nails
13 Rx-writers' org.
14 Beaver's project
15 Shows amusement
16 Thoreau : David :: Emerson : —
17 Arrivederci, in Avignon
18 Intended
24 Insalata Caprese ingredient
25 Sommer of filmdom
29 Rubbed out
31 RPM gauges
32 On the briny
33 Genesis creation
34 "— Said" (Neil Diamond hit)
35 Some sports prizes
36 Border on
37 Membership list
38 Sweetheart
40 Noisy crier
43 Strips cut by mowing
45 Dealer in hot goods
46 That, in a bodega
47 Each letter of Roy G. Biv
48 Air freshener targets
49 Org. against fur-wearing
51 Evening, in ads
52 Used a dressage gait
53 "What — God wrought?"
58 More haunting
60 Gibbon, e.g.
62 Housetop stories
63 Salt Lake City athlete
64 Impel
65 *Not like this*
66 Lhasa — (Tibetan dogs)
67 What Eeyore loses and gets back
68 Actress Blair et al.
69 "Indeed, old chap!"
70 Trudge
74 Hidden cache
75 Inarticulate hesitations
76 Like — out of water
78 Zeus, as a swan, seduced her
79 French singles
80 Benchmarks: abbr.
82 Setbacks for dieters
83 Give off
84 Suffix with psych
85 1931 Dracula portrayer
90 Friars Club affairs
91 Part of USPS
92 Heady thrill
93 Bread baking supplies
95 Memory slip
96 Eating place in "Eat Pray Love"
97 Borden "spokescow"
98 Spritelike
99 Terra — (reddish-brown)
101 Aggressive in personality
104 Judicial order
105 Age after Bronze
106 Seedy joint
107 When the French fry?
108 Nine-digit IDs
110 Clinton's Buddy was a choc. one
111 All — day's work
112 Slipperiness exemplar
113 Worldwide workers' grp.

Turnabout Is Fair Play

Across

1 Nosh under lox
6 Spy sent by Moses to Canaan
11 Drug-busting cop
15 Clickable address
18 Stubborn as ——
19 Steer clear of
20 Cognizant
22 Baby's dovelike sound
23 Highland wear
24 Fabled reporter of a "current" event?
27 Hockey's Phil, familiarly
28 One in a pizzeria's name
29 Sans siblings
30 Widen, as pupils
31 Sheik's bevy
34 Ninny
36 Explorer Hernando de ——
37 Trio of trios
39 Undesirable place to stay?
45 Teeny amount
47 Kvetch
49 Makeshift shelter
50 Comic actress Martha
51 iPhone download
52 Puppet pal of Kukla
54 Small suitcase
57 Fury
58 "This brew is just as good as the regular," maybe?
62 Fairy tale dwellings
64 Loudly sound
65 Hurried away
66 Hits "send," maybe
68 Fluctuate markedly
69 How the Scarecrow wanted to be accepted?
72 At a distance
76 Like some yowling calicoes
78 Locks
79 Jong with "Fear of Fifty"
80 Venison source
83 Blistering angry rebuff?
86 Its cap. is Abu Dhabi
87 Stephen King debut novel
90 Big books
91 Soft & —— (deodorant brand)
92 Homer Simpson's beer
94 Before the deadline
97 Ending with silver or stone
98 Creator of James and M
99 For barbers, they're intense?
103 Improperly long sentence
105 "Believe —— not!"
106 Morales of "La Bamba"
107 Amalgamate
109 Grammy winner Yearwood
112 Window framework
114 "Illmatic" rapper
117 "Julie & Julia" director Ephron
119 Risk falling during a fruiteating binge?
122 Zester target
123 Drips in ERs
124 Wood for chests
125 "Crocodile Hunter" Steve
126 A macaroni penguin's is yellow
127 Often-hot spot, for a Scot
128 Bank takeback, briefly
129 Causes for cramming
130 Force units

Down

1 Use a tandoor
2 Low-tech sect
3 User-friendly, à la beer pong?
4 La corrida charger
5 Article in Arles, literally
6 Philippine island ("cube" anagram)
7 Mary Kay competitor
8 Let go for lack of work
9 A brother of Robt. Kennedy
10 Be incumbent upon
11 Table salt, in chem class
12 Out of whack
13 Bollywood actress Aishwarya
14 Beliefs
15 Pac-10 sch. of the Bruins
16 Cheer (for)
17 "The West Wing" actor Rob
21 Pulitzer-winning Wharton
25 Absent with permission
26 Inside story?
32 Make cryptic
33 Country's Travis or Haggard
35 Kind of slick
36 Exhibiting no emotion
38 Soothing powder
40 Genetic info carrier
41 View from The Hamptons: abbr.
42 Opossum's gripper
43 A Brontë title heroine
44 Dregs
45 Striped kitty
46 Speed skater —— Anton Ohno
48 Breakaway state from Nigeria, 1967–70
53 Key of Beethoven's "Eroica"
55 Spanker or spinnaker
56 Subj. for new citizens
59 Bot such as R2-D2
60 Ayres who played "Dr. Kildare"
61 Montana neighbor
63 Autocrats
66 Royal decree
67 Bone cavity tissue
69 Bygone diamond of Queens
70 Yorkie or Scottie
71 D. C. ballplayer, briefly
73 "Harbinger Hunt: The Movie"?
74 High-end Honda division
75 Peace Prize co-winner Yitzhak
77 Tokyo-based computer co.
79 Ancient Jewish ascetic
80 Insolent
81 French waters
82 Nimble
83 Paris Hilton, e.g.
84 Epps of "House"
85 Immunization fluid
88 They hook up 123-Across
89 Addams Family's Cousin ——
93 Pat down
95 Slam-dancing site
96 Ecol. watchdog grp.
100 Value system
101 Kvetcher
102 Figurative sources of strength
104 Cantankerous
108 Jagged, as leaf edges
109 Annoying person
110 Glowing review
111 Rick's "Casablanca" love
112 No-brainer
113 Prefix with sol or drome
115 Touched down
116 Nine-digit IDs
118 Tiny toilers
120 Pindaric poem
121 Afore
122 HDTV screen type

23

Broadway Runs

Across

1 Childe with paintings in The Met
7 "Star Wars" knight
11 Unwelcome word from 72-Across
15 Hamlet, e.g.
19 Julia's "Seinfeld" role
20 Chief Norse god
21 Switcheroo
22 Truant G.I.
23 Nasty number of baseball players curse an American League team (2003, 1982, 1955)
27 "Parsley is gharsley" poet
28 Coney Island's —— Park
29 Sci-fi sightings
30 Ramen morsel
31 A-line line
32 "Oh, woe!"
33 Med. sch. class
34 Garden State youth use pomade (2005, 1972, 1968)
43 Credit groups, maybe
44 Gondolier's handful
45 Some TV screens
46 Kan. neighbor
48 Togs
49 Drops on fields
50 Vivacity
52 D-Day invasion town
53 Female heartthrobs don't believe one maven (1981, 2005, 1975)
60 It's directed to Sun. worshippers
61 Draft status
62 Human trunks
63 Highly ornate style
64 U.S. island east of the Philippines
65 Symbol of achievement
66 Pairs
67 Bible book after Acts
70 Hulking
71 Part of CD or D.J.
72 Tax prep VIP
75 Detective cordons off a hazardous site (1970, 1987, 1978)
79 Saltimbocca meat
80 Asian nanny
81 Hostel relative
82 Polishes, say
83 —— squared (circle area calculation)
84 "The Iron Chancellor" von Bismarck
86 Undesirable freshness
88 Crinkly fabric
90 Cool people have apartments atop Manhattan hills (1982, 1996, 2008)
95 Just slightly
96 Missouri River tribe
97 Curtains, so to speak
98 President —— (acting leader)
101 Pack away
102 Not rot
104 Parable or fable
108 We villagers are able to ax unwanted e-mail often (1938, 1953, 2005)
112 Miscellany
113 Shrinking Asian sea
114 Cockeyed
115 Pertaining to milk
116 O'Brien's predecessor and successor
117 Thanksgiving tubers
118 Sympathetic compassion
119 Rustling sound

Down

1 Given the ax?
2 Inter —— (among other things)
3 Pouches such as bursae
4 Turban-wearing Punjabi, perhaps
5 Meth or pent suffix
6 Musical miscellanies
7 Solder
8 "Show Boat" author Ferber
9 Cube with pips
10 Gratify
11 Diffuse through a membrane
12 Has
13 You might do it dearly
14 Bridged
15 The ——, famed Manhattan residence
16 Wonder-struck
17 Coward knighted in 1970
18 Alternatively
24 Under a local
25 Miles away
26 —— Ark
31 "Not I" addressee
32 Communication at Gallaudet U.
33 "My Fair Lady" race place
34 Their debut album was "Wynonna and Naomi"
35 Accustom
36 Straphanger
37 Slugger Sammy
38 What Broadway's "Aida" was not
39 Distressed scream
40 Out, of sorts
41 The way a bagel is often cut
42 Dig find
47 Nincompoop
49 Word with carpe or per
50 Argentine writer of "Ficciones"
51 Stratagem
52 An hr. has 360
54 Hop atop
55 Grind together
56 Sago, for instance
57 Sidestep
58 "—— one who has gone through it" (Virgil)
59 It may be rotgut
64 Ancient France
65 "Munich" star Eric
66 Gorilla researcher Fossey
67 "Let me know" letters
68 Type of acid in soaps
69 Stiller's comedy partner
70 Wheels of misfortune?
71 Thickheaded
72 Do compacting
73 Milwaukee theater named for a brewer
74 Basilica sections
76 In the cards
77 Ramekin, e.g.
78 Subj. that uses sine language
84 Lead-in to arthritis or porosis
85 Manhattan–Roosevelt Island conveyance
86 High peak topper
87 Had shad
88 Friends via snail mail
89 Steam cooker part
91 Art under wraps, perhaps
92 Bottom lines
93 Lay —— the line
94 Dickens's Uriah
98 Where laps are wet
99 Hold sway
100 "Little Shop of Horrors" dentist
101 Hoodwink
102 Classical pretzel shape
103 Annual TV sports award
104 It may be soft-shelled
105 Kind of clef
106 Comic strip partner of Hi
107 Create some intaglio
109 Org. Heston headed
110 Thrilla in Manila boxer
111 Animal's mouth

24

For Fun

Across

1 Psyched (up)
6 Uplifting lingerie
10 Etna ejecta
14 Nudnik
18 Keanu of "Constantine"
20 Witness-stand pledge
21 Fateful March date
22 Friend in war
23 Simply lettered "Welcome" or "Wipe Your Paws"?
26 Film-trailer segment
27 Hercules slew the Nemean one
28 Bone in a cage
29 Welcome words on a flight board
31 Greek X
34 Hardly modern, as far as locks of hair are concerned?
40 Football powwow formation
42 Belted, in the Bible
43 Vittles
44 Fruit with wrinkly skin
45 Student of Socrates
46 Weight-training lifts
50 Is enthusiastic about senescence?
54 Muslim holiday
55 "Star Wars" baddie Jabba the —
57 Bodies of laws or literature
58 Norway's patron saint
60 French city, in song
61 Ear: prefix
64 Comedian Foxx
65 What a friend of Mr. Cleaver might do, regarding his tab?
68 Sunscreen option
70 Black-eyed —
71 Depended
72 Of melodic benefit?
75 It's on the house
77 Actress Myrna
78 Emotionally remote
79 Father of explorer Leif
80 "The Family Circus" cartoonist's family
82 Peddle
83 J. Alfred Prufrock poet's initials
84 Custom of the retired hoopster Yao?
90 Napoleon fiancée and 1954 Jean Simmons film
92 Hayworth and Moreno
93 Person logging in
94 Hand, in Juárez
95 Fireplace remnant
96 Specialty of "The Onion"
98 Like some clickable buttons on auction websites?
104 Boar's mate
105 The Coneheads, e.g.
106 "Glee" actress — Michele
107 Like an ungracious loser
109 Star-guided trio
110 Discovery of benefit to a napper?
119 Kuwaiti ruler
120 Emmy-winning Falco
121 Spot for a nosh
122 Got misty with emotion
123 Value-meal drink
124 Sound of many fans
125 Motown music category
126 Honor-defending showdowns

Down

1 Dada-movement artist
2 Funnyman Brooks
3 Black-eyed —
4 Depraved
5 Common response to loss
6 Kind of pleat or seat
7 Snitch
8 Raiders from the Justice Dept.
9 Weight with a heavier British counterpart
10 State of uncertainty
11 Grp. advocating flossing
12 Doc of the bay?
13 Varied
14 Formal agreements
15 With 35-Down, Immigration Museum site
16 Gross goo
17 Varieties
19 Monolith material
24 Business-letter abbr.
25 Abounding
30 Nemesis of Capone
31 Guzzle
32 "Les Misérables" author Victor
33 Doing nothing
35 See 15-Down
36 Web 'zines
37 Reply to the Little Red Hen
38 Echo
39 Import tax
41 Part of CD or D.J.
45 Goad
47 Shoulder wrap
48 Train-pass provider abroad
49 Audio system
51 Distant
52 Bridge player's opener, briefly
53 Some Prado paintings
56 Huggable kind of bear
59 Vietnam Memorial architect Maya
60 Like better
61 Gymnast Korbut et al.
62 Drove (around)
63 "Lawrence of Arabia" star Peter
65 Drink served from a bowl
66 Enzyme suffix
67 University of Maine's home
69 Folks with many fans
70 Fashion designer Anna
73 Transmit again
74 2011 film "The — Life"
75 Hinder
76 Lummoxes
80 Falsified, as a check
81 Lewd material
83 Switch colleges, say
85 Sleeve-encircling symbols
86 Netanyahu nickname
87 Egyptian fertility goddess
88 Whodunit character Wolfe
89 Cultivated
91 One-named former supermodel
95 "... — saw Elba" (palindrome part)
96 Quickly downed shot
97 Jibed
98 Titled women such as Helen Mirren
99 San Antonio landmark
100 Inflexible
101 "Atonement" star Knightley
102 More mature, maybe
103 Where Peres is pres.
108 Genesis twin
111 Nuptial agreement
112 Actress Vardalos
113 It made Prizms and Trackers
114 Nasty viral bug
115 Manet medium
116 Quattro preceder
117 Snakelike fish
118 Hwys.

MediCine

Across

1 Credit-union offering
5 Handel contemporary
9 Timbuktu's country
13 Digging tool
18 Effect used in ultrasound tests
19 Realty measure
20 Confronted
21 Hospital staffers
22 "What did you first learn in med school, doc?" "___" (2000)
25 Grows dim
26 401(k) kin
27 Dance move
28 One of LBJ's daughters
29 "The Raven" maiden
30 Calm with drugs, say
32 "Did you have a favorite anatomy topic?" "___" (2009)
36 Grown filly
38 Fall mos.
39 Queen Margrethe's subjects
40 Walk pompously
43 Shed, as skin
45 Color just a touch
46 Tease
49 "Which case took you the longest to remedy?" "___" (1955)
53 Clownish type
54 Top-drawer
55 "You ___ here"
56 Go by, as time
57 Tennis ___ (joint condition)
58 Wish undone
59 Compadre
61 ___ Friday's (eatery chain)
62 I.V. contents
63 "What's that patient's car crash injury?" "___ (2014)...
66 ...but luckily his neck was ___" (2014)
69 Indoor flight, maybe
71 Lid
73 Dr. whose books aren't medical
74 Medical kind of scan
77 Cuba ___ (rum drink)
78 Gomer Pyle exclamation
81 Birth-announcement abbr.
82 Equestrian sport
83 Eye wolfishly
84 "Tell me about working in the E.R." "___" (2007)
87 Drone, e.g.
88 Un + deux
89 Barking swimmer
90 Freed of leaves
91 Sweeties
92 Dell
94 Neck and neck
96 "You're often on call at night". "Yep, I've given many ___" (1964)
101 First-year resident, once
105 Deteriorated condition
106 Part of M*A*S*H
107 In traction, e.g.
109 Poseidon's realm
110 Spree
111 "What's that procedure you're doing? "___" (1984)
115 Lawn-trimming tool
116 Unisex flat hat
117 Atop
118 Skunk toon Le Pew
119 Navel orange's lack
120 1974 CIA film spoof
121 Org. operating Curiosity
122 Capone pursuer

Down

1 Carroll who wrote about Alice
2 Earthy colour
3 In the lead
4 ___'easter
5 Cake-making mixture
6 Arthritis symptom
7 Moved stealthily
8 Snicker sound
9 Infamous Imelda or Ferdinand
10 Play part, perhaps
11 Waikiki keepsake
12 Hosp. wristbands, e.g.
13 Low-risk wager
14 Some uprights
15 Extra feature
16 Big name in tractors
17 Trio of diseases?
20 Fracture of geological concern
23 Will subject
24 Vote winner
29 Attorney General Loretta
31 Make smile
33 Sacred
34 Does cutting-room work
35 Simpson-trial judge Ito
37 Chef Lagasse
40 Lead in a cast
41 10 C-Notes
42 Like solar energy
44 Russian lake ("Genoa" anagram)
45 Easy hoops moves
46 "Coma" author
47 Former Lacoste partner
48 Bends at shows' ends
50 Top parts of shoes
51 In-flight height: abbr.
52 Pasta-sauce brand
53 Emergency-code color
57 Fraternal-lodge members
59 Suffix with billion
60 "The English Patient" won nine
62 "Lenny" director Bob
64 Bring on staff
65 Initiate, as pledges
67 "Twilight" lead role for Kristen
68 Demolition debris
69 No neatnik
70 Buster Brown's pooch
72 Bear foot
75 Botanical burn-soother
76 Sondheim title barber
78 Given a "woolcut"
79 Bank robbery
80 Loses temporarily
82 It may be medicinal
84 Distinguishing feature
85 Sinister glance
86 Rhoda's sister on "Rhoda"
88 Restrains with chains, say
91 Followed relentlessly
92 Bible divisions
93 Accept as an inpatient
95 Austrian "City of Music"
96 French clerics
97 Chute
98 Door pivot
99 Apelike, in a way
100 Iota follower
102 First name in cosmetics
103 Gains grains
104 Scruffs
108 Life-story recaps
111 "Very funny" TV sta.
112 With it, old-style
113 Common cause of burns
114 Hosp. staffer

Med School Caper

Across

1 Shaker made from a gourd
7 Creator of Athos, Porthos, and Aramis
12 Bistro waiter
18 Locust-like insects
19 California wine valley
20 Loath
21 Basic lecture topic for internists-to-be?
23 Summer airing, often
24 Luxe
25 Get bushed
26 What orthopedics students do?
28 Least frequent
30 Celtic one-named singer
31 —— mater
32 Blinded Biblical strongman
36 Anterior
38 Time delays
40 Cut-rate, in commercial names
41 Colonial news source
43 It has two banks in Paris?
45 Bewildered condition
48 When obstetrics students really have to deliver?
51 Weapon in Clue
53 Harts and hinds
54 Huge Brit. lexicon
55 Some Nice seasons
57 Posthumously crowned Portuguese queen
58 Julian Assange's revelations
60 Ralph of Polo fame
63 "Toxic" singer
65 Easy mark
67 What all med students get in "End-of-Life Care"?
70 Tai neighbor
71 Socially restrictive
73 "My Antonia" author
74 A-list
76 Bad word to hear in the O.R.
77 Adriatic port of Italy
78 Role in "Exodus" and "Entourage"
79 Graph line
82 Noted mother-painter
85 Surgery 101?
90 Gal of song
91 Pulitzer-winning composer Ned
93 You can cool or dig them in
94 One of "The Simpsons"
95 One of "The Simpsons"
96 Job hunter's achievement
98 Past and future, e.g.
99 Swine swill
101 Starchy tropical tuber
103 "—— Joe" (boxer Frazier)
106 Removable section of a surgery textbook?
109 Decrease?
110 Manhattan Chinatown street
114 Former Mrs. Mandela
115 Med student's tool for calculating dosages?
118 Purpose
119 Kind of skates
120 Crisscross pattern
121 Queen Elizabeth II's predecessor
122 "All About ——" (2009 film flop)
123 Grab

Down

1 Japanese soup choice
2 Unreturnable serves
3 Dermatologist's type of decision?
4 Commotion
5 Loose cover-up
6 Up and about
7 Rx writer
8 Some, in Spain
9 Like lava
10 Dosages
11 "Annie" pooch
12 Scrubs, for instance
13 Had a mean value of
14 Disgusts
15 Carbonara sauce ingredient
16 Honshu metropolis
17 Knicks' rivals
18 Many a trophy
19 Deems it appropriate (to)
22 Otto I's realm: abbr.
27 Undergrads with pediatrician Spock
28 Hospital helipad site
29 Outdoor surgery "patient"?
32 Pip
33 Bad marks students may get?
34 Feature of ophthalmology students' lab?
35 Common sleep apnea symptom
37 Bobby in hockey history
39 "Ugly Betty" actress Ortiz
41 Deep Blue's game
42 Carmine
44 Supreme Court Justice Kagan
45 Future coroners are never done with them?
46 Met presentation
47 Bas-relief mixture
49 Sweet Hungarian wine
50 Blend in, on a road sign
52 Chart type
56 Guam, e.g.: abbr.
59 NYPD alert
60 Perjurer
61 Shenanigan
62 "That's gross!"
63 Baseball bigwig Bud
64 Greek letter/Neptune symbol
65 Flat-bottomed boats
66 "Ciao!," at a luau
68 Cause to start
69 Laura and Bruce in acting
72 Some pre-med degs.
75 Raptor's grasper
77 Dress down
78 Need 7-Down, maybe
80 Words akin to a nod
81 Lith. and Ukr., once
83 Emulating Dr. Leary
84 Part of UCLA
86 TV broadcasting band
87 Casual tops
88 One who eats at home?
89 Julie of "The Early Show"
92 Bitingly sarcastic
95 Body shop amenity
97 Human flaw
98 Fictional heart seeker
99 Excel
100 Slowly, musically
102 Those opposed
104 Tolkien humanoid
105 Some menthol smokes
106 Tiny branch
107 Sampras or Seeger
108 CCXX ÷ V
110 Hardly a designer dog
111 Ear-related
112 Part of SUNY's F.I.T.
113 Quattro preceder
116 Nashville-to-NYC dir.
117 Org. for home-school ties

Letter Play

Across

1 Concerning
5 Formal-invitation information
11 Like some exams
15 Peak point
19 Insignificant variation
20 Zero with three Tonys
21 Divide by ordinance, perhaps
22 Tibia's place
23 HANG?
26 Former days
27 Based on hypothesis
28 Corn Belt state
29 Castaway's spot
30 Solidifies
31 DI?
38 Threw away
40 Make it
41 Surpassed in a dash
45 Maharani wraps
48 "Strange Magic" rock grp.
49 Balm botanical
50 TEN?
58 Meets with boats
60 Ghostly visitor to Scrooge
61 Person logging in
62 "Wolf!" crier, at times
63 Legally invalid
64 Structure with a keep
66 VIN?
72 BET?
74 "That's certainly apparent to me"
75 Emmy-winning Banks
77 WWII General Bradley
78 Apart from this
79 "Six Feet Under" star Peter
81 One of South Africa's capitals
85 AREA?
89 No more than
90 Actress Salonga or Michele
91 Raptor's grasper
92 Steamed Mexican dish
94 Biblical cry of praise
98 Raphael, for one
100 NERO?
104 ___ S. Connell, creator of Mr. and Mrs. Bridge
108 "In the style of", Italian-style
109 Muse of history
110 Slapstick trio of yore
113 One might be apparent
114 OR?
119 Last Stuart queen
120 Carmaking contemporary of Daimler
121 Withstand
122 A deadly sin
123 Scholarship criterion
124 What some call their pop
125 Belts of booze
126 Batik supplies

Down

1 Palindromic pop-group name
2 Lingerie items
3 Big cat, in Cannes
4 Footnote kin of ibid.
5 Sino-Russian border river
6 Mixers with gin or vodka
7 Sound of reproach
8 Skater Midori
9 One may OK a KO
10 Spanish folk hero
11 Conductor Seiji
12 "Brooklyn" star Saoirse and family
13 With 14-Down, "Life of Pi" director
14 See above
15 Have high hopes
16 Like a virgin
17 Deceived
18 Add to a spreadsheet, say
24 Ornamental with showy leaves
25 ___ polloi
32 Orgs.
33 Hardly slovenly
34 To the point, in law
35 Seek information from
36 Bruins' sch.
37 Just ___ in the wheel (one with a small role)
39 Performing in the theater
41 Dinghy mover
42 Suffix with glob
43 Dress (up)
44 Comes to understand, British-style
46 Put ___ appearance
47 Prep before operating
51 Tombstone lawman
52 Fanning of "20th Century Women"
53 Fedora fabric
54 Chicken marsala tidbit
55 "¿Cómo ___ usted?"
56 Dudley Do-Right's love
57 Not kosher
59 Fork prong
64 Solidifies
65 "I smell ___!"
66 Fraction of a min.
67 "Return of the Jedi" slave-dancer
68 Carpentry clamp
69 Gillette razor brand
70 Nolan with seven no-hitters
71 Deem reliable
73 Corrida charger
76 Cruising, maybe
79 Reeves of "Speed"
80 Razzle-dazzle
81 Broadly spotted horse
82 Messenger molecule letters
83 Green around the gills
84 "Yes, Captain!"
86 Banned fruit spray
87 Nevada gambling mecca
88 Singer Amos born Myra
93 Took tastes from, biblically
94 Abductee of Paris, in Paris
95 Egosurfing, say
96 Browned quickly, as tuna
97 Go up
99 Do what a caret indicates
100 Longtime "Playboy" cartoonist ___ Wilson
101 Hotel home of "Eloise"
102 Manet medium
103 (The) things newbies must learn
105 Pledged
106 Intense suffering
107 Temerity
111 Wings tips' tips
112 "The ___ the limit!"
114 Six-pack muscles
115 Vintage car monogram
116 Bed-and-breakfast alternative
117 Tokyo, once
118 Mongrel

Wear to Eat

Across

1 Skin layer
7 "Mamma Mia!" pop group
11 Discreet summons
15 YouTube offering
19 Fictional Plaza Hotel imp
20 Simon, creator of Oscar and Felix
21 ___ mater
22 Ascend
23 Wear to eat?
25 Mixture in many French sauces
26 Competent
27 Map detail
28 "Zip-___-Doo-Dah"
29 Wear to eat?
31 Be in accord
33 Huge Brit. lexicon
34 Major putdowns
35 Wear to eat?
40 Café lightener
43 Counting everything
44 Solid downpour
45 "___ Lee" (Poe poem)
49 ___ Lee (comic-book writer)
50 Spearheaded
52 Wear to eat?
55 Like Spanish roofs, often
57 Overnight drops
59 Sphere head?
60 Pond organism
61 Infrequently
63 Fruit with custardy flesh
67 Attaches, as some patches
69 Wear to eat?
72 ChapStick or Blistex
76 Renée of silents
77 Filmdom's Martin and Charlie
82 Butter sub
83 Pet-food brand
85 Snitch
87 Golfer Palmer, familiarly
88 Wear to eat?
93 Pen point
95 "Picnic" playwright
96 Feels indignant about
97 Darth's daughter
99 Delivered from danger
101 Part of PDA
102 Wear to eat?
104 Keys in seas
108 There's something in the way she moos?
109 Grasslike marsh plant
110 Wear to eat?
114 Digital-camera mode
115 Cell-phone giant
120 Tibetan priest
121 Land of Shiraz
122 What to do with wear to eat?
124 Suffix with sinus
125 Hardly a jock
126 Olympics gymnast Korbut
127 "Gangsta's Paradise" rapper
128 "Our Gang" pup
129 Catch a glimpse of
130 Sought damages
131 Gofer's task

Down

1 "Entourage" actress Mazar
2 North Carolina campus
3 Competes at Henley
4 Tick's tiny cousin
5 "Visually fun, but … museum worthy?"
6 Witness
7 Ancient head garland
8 Implore
9 Take the bait
10 Menu phrase
11 Whittled (down)
12 Trudge
13 Cockily self-satisfied
14 Airport limo alternative
15 Rush-hour pace
16 Columbus Day baby's sign
17 Faith with Five Pillars
18 Friends, slangily
24 Let a con out of the can early
29 Reims's river ("elves" anagram)
30 Cornerstone abbr.
32 Desired outcome
33 TV boy from Mayberry
35 Fine sprays
36 Set free, in a way
37 Play for time
38 Sharpened
39 Contented sigh
40 Hold up
41 Word-finding deficit
42 Tips off
46 Dietary-fiber source
47 Morays and congers
48 Italia's Garda or Como, e.g.
51 Captain Sparrow portrayer
53 Howard Cosell was once one
54 Veep before Al
56 "David Copperfield" wife
58 "The ___ Cannonball"
62 Disparages
64 Joined at the chuppah
65 Whiz
66 Departure's opp.
68 Govt. workplace watchdog
70 Slangy savvy
71 Archie: Carroll :: Edith: ___
72 Home builder's buy
73 A.J. Soprano portrayer Robert
74 Ending meaning "foot"
75 Physiques, in muscle mags
78 Author Jong
79 Listlessness
80 Bruce who played Watson
81 Begonias' beginnings
84 It's square-rigged on a brig
86 Fed up with
89 Bread baker's need
90 Completely hunky-dory
91 "Want Whiskas now!"
92 Bro or sis
94 The Titanic's undoing
98 Mitigate
100 Speaker with a booming voice
103 Foursome
104 Long Island South Shore town
105 Do toe loops and lutzes
106 Restrict
107 Rub out
108 Dum Dums and Dots
111 Trigonometric ratio
112 Uno + dos
113 Tombstone lawman
114 Human-rights org.
116 It may be fishy
117 Caffeine-rich kind of nut
118 "Checkmate!"
119 "And giving ___, up the chimney…"
122 Song from 7-Across
123 Rub out

Bollywood Titles

Across

1 Trapper's prize
5 Train for a bout
9 Music's Aimee and Herbie
14 Cup for café, say
19 Missouri River tribe
20 Top-rated
21 Actress Bingham or Lords
22 Faith with Five Pillars
23 Fairy tale set atop Indian cloth? (2005)
26 Sphere of influence
27 Hindu ascetic
28 Fury
29 No more stigmatized social class in India? (2000)
31 Mail recipient
33 Came to rest
36 Veer off course
37 Men with Indian legume mixtures? (1955)
41 Raid targets
45 Bill Nye's subj.
48 Aliens in UFOs, e.g.
49 Letter-shaped girder
51 Main vessel from the heart
53 Fivesome
56 Blessedly mild products of Indian baking? (1983)
60 Chamber-music grouping
61 South African native
62 First name in Al Qaeda history
63 —— culpa
64 Land, to Livy
65 One day at ——
67 Some rental trucks
70 No amount of Indian money will cover the cost? (1998)
76 World's largest country
78 Immunization fluid
79 Do a tailoring job
82 Toronto's prov.
83 Jazz trumpeter Davis
88 Frolic
89 Carell in comic roles
90 Have you considered Indian food-on-a-stick? (1991)
94 Rubbernecked
95 Lutelike Indian instrument
96 Up to the point when
97 Chinese philosopher —— Tzu
99 Next yr.'s alums
100 Long-lasting dos
102 Indian religious concept meets doomsday? (1998)
107 "Ciao!"
109 Cantina tidbit
110 Asian tiered tower
113 Indian version of "The King and I"? (1989)
119 Director Kazan
121 Utah city near Sundance
123 Set straight
124 This Indian dress is not what I wanted? (1948)
128 Gave in
129 Put on cloud nine
130 Cookie since 1912
131 Billion ending
132 Genuflection joints
133 Aids to getting organized
134 Quiz
135 Minus

Down

1 Magician's "It's vanished!"
2 Old lab burners
3 English philosopher John
4 —— off (starting, in golf)
5 Easy mark
6 Most needy
7 Oscar winner Paquin
8 President nicknamed "Dutch"
9 LIRR's "parent"
10 Suffix with drunk or tank
11 Pusher buster
12 Campus sports org.
13 Hollywood's Spacek
14 What a tread-depth gauge checks
15 Cruising, maybe
16 Deli side dish
17 Hacienda room
18 Small-screen award
24 Language related to Hindi
25 Canasta objective
30 Emulate Mumbles in "Happy Feet"
32 Ogled
34 "What —— for Love"
35 Verboten
38 Sharp as a tack
39 Some summer babies
40 "Roseanne" actress Gilbert
42 Part of ASCAP or ASPCA: abbr.
43 School-year divisions, perhaps
44 Take the helm
45 Catch sight of
46 Gospel singer Winans
47 Like commerce within Ohio, e.g.
50 "Dee-lish!"
52 Botanist Gray, et al.
54 U. of Maryland players, briefly
55 Video-game pioneer
57 Shawkat of "Arrested Development"
58 Under a local
59 O.K. Corral lawman
61 Efron of "High School Musical"
66 Dawn deity
68 Leavening agent
69 Gamma follower
71 Foot in some poems
72 It's conjugated
73 Ending for switch
74 Sound of distant thunder
75 Strike caller
76 Competes at Henley
77 Nerdy
80 Always
81 Malbec, Médoc, etc.
84 Promissory note
85 Knucklehead
86 Blues singer James
87 Sarong, e.g.
91 Sailor
92 Strips encircling sleeves
93 —— mater
94 Float ingredient
98 Mag revenue sources
101 Thesaurus entry: abbr.
103 Copycat
104 Big oaf
105 KGB forerunner
106 Standard
108 1950s Ford flop
111 Teen Gillis of old TV
112 States firmly
113 Dress-shop fixture
114 Economist Greenspan
115 Jazz jargon
116 Posthumous Pulitzer winner James
117 Timbuktu's country
118 Periods given names
120 Legal memo phrase
122 Lode loads
125 Cousin on "The Addams Family"
126 "The Darjeeling Limited" director Anderson
127 "Just kidding!"

Speak-k Easy

Across

1 Campus digs
5 Dell
9 Warring Olympian
13 Oil-yielding rock
18 More than passed
19 Trigger : Rogers :: Buttermilk : __
21 Precious prefix
22 Firmed at the gym
23 "What I'm holding is more like a nest than a mug!"?
26 Make corrections to
27 Squeaky shriek
28 Reformer-journalist Jacob
29 Great Lakes' __ Canals
30 Elbow room, so to speak
31 Gross-sounding advice for treating a cold?
37 Scotland's Skye, e.g.
38 Objectivist writer Rand
39 Some come from a drum
40 Initials of toy retailer Schwarz
43 Blueprint
46 River of central Germany
48 New Rochelle home of the Gaels
49 Willowy
50 Classroom worker
51 Dessert that causes indigestion?
56 Drink from leaves
57 Jai __ (court sport)
60 Vintage auto monogram
61 Like the "Coneheads"
62 Game bird with a spine abnormality?
66 Pubs
68 Start of Juliet's balcony cry
69 Mr. Clean Magic __ (scrubbing aid)
71 Cynical writer Bierce
74 Dress a young fox to look dapper?
81 New York's is "Excelsior"
82 Glass rim
83 D.C. ballplayers
84 R&B's Rawls
85 Phase during which you could destroy the relatives?
91 Effrontery
92 List-ending abbr.
93 Take to the cleaners
94 Furtive "Hey, you!"
97 Former Yankee Sparky
98 Sleep-lab letters
99 More rational
100 Kind of cap
102 Mafia boss
104 Enjoy seeing a profanity while reading social media?
110 Italian sub layer
113 Part-goat Greek god
114 Folies-Bergère set designer
115 Baton Rouge sch.
116 Suspect's way out
117 "Iron Man" Tony with a yen for a satirical magazine?
122 Dreidel letter
123 Lei Day dance
124 Monopoly buy
125 Italia's __ di Como
126 Pilfered
127 Escape route
128 To be, at the Forum
129 Bills in tills

Down

1 Passé
2 Earthy pigment
3 Japanese healing practice
4 OBs and GPs
5 Small anatomical sac
6 Was of use
7 Wonder Woman's golden weapon
8 Tolkien tree creature
9 Request from
10 Camcorder button
11 Outback bird
12 Thimbleful
13 Knights' mounts
14 Domiciles
15 Over again
16 Dunham of HBO's "Girls"
17 Whirling current
20 Hollywood's Spacek
24 Annoys
25 Maine __ cat
30 Pale purple
32 Low card in pinochle
33 Scarlett's home
34 Cold, in Colombia
35 Its "fruit" is high-fiber
36 Radius neighbor
40 Knack
41 Writer Conrad or singer Clay
42 Prophetic signs
43 Course toward a goal
44 Stead
45 Genesis front man?
47 Moped's greener cousin
49 White of the eye
52 R & B group __ Hill
53 Coral habitat
54 French pronoun
55 Sites of sanctuary
57 Robert Frost's "__ in the City"
58 It's east of Thailand
59 Pinnacle
63 Imposing entrance
64 Shia holy city in Iran
65 Albanian currency
66 Brit's "Ciao!"
67 Prof's TA, say
70 They make twists
71 Grainfield hue
72 Death, in Venice
73 Second-string crew
75 Glass of Bass
76 White-wine aperitif
77 Prefix with dermis or dural
78 Wendy Wasserstein work
79 Inquiry from Pew Research, e.g.
80 Eggnog season
86 Military-uniform cloth
87 Actress Skye
88 Minute minute fraction: abbr.
89 Lake Titicaca borders it
90 Begin the bidding
91 Squishy lump
95 Neck wraps
96 Perceptible by touch
99 "Red as a beet", for instance
100 "Out of Africa" author Dinesen
101 Large spiral seashell
103 Rounded hammer part
104 Decca or EMI
105 Fat-forgoer of rhyme
106 Tours de force
107 "__ River" ("Show Boat" song)
108 Missouri river or tribe
109 Accolades
110 Droops
111 Came to rest
112 Prom rental
117 Yonder yacht
118 Prom rental
119 Actor Mahershala
120 Caviar base
121 Day-__ Color Corp.

Tiger Mother

Across

1 NYC subway debut of 1904
4 Confucian path
7 "The Jungle Book" bear
12 Acid neutralizer
18 1988 remake starring Quaid and Ryan
19 Drudgery
20 Alda and Arkin
21 Transferred, as a house title
22 Mother is strict! She expects us to —
25 Window smasher, e.g.
26 Pay to play, in a way
27 List of corrections
28 Craze
29 Blue shade
30 Novelist Graham
32 Gas rating number
34 Thistlelike plant
36 We're so tired! We always have to —
43 Riverbank deposit
44 They punctuate analogies
46 Road map abbr.
47 Qatar's capital
48 No "people food" for us. We never get to —
51 Parts of overalls
52 Saharan
53 Ill temper
54 Took the train
55 Salad fish
56 Frazier competitor
57 Barnard's upstate sister
59 When we ask what's for dinner, she says we're —
66 Astounds
68 Put forth, as a theory
69 Stay fresh
70 She scares us out of having seconds by saying, "—!"
75 Obscene
79 Massachusetts cape
80 Actress Charlotte et al.
81 Each, informally
83 Acapulco gold
84 Tara of "American Pie"
86 Gung-ho
87 To help her keep tabs on us, she hired a —
91 It may be blind
92 A Bobbsey twin
93 More optimistic
94 Mozartian article
95 Slumber parties? We aren't even allowed to —
98 Embellished a résumé, say
101 High regard
102 Prefix meaning stomach
104 Pampering setting
107 — Moines, Iowa
108 Playsuit
111 Pokes fun at
115 Tiger kitty, maybe
117 When we got our fur dirty, she sure —
119 Consecrate with oil
120 Fake-fat brand
121 Call's partner
122 Blotto
123 Chew out
124 "Strange to say . . ."
125 Neptune's realm
126 Goes too far on the meds

Down

1 Creative seed
2 Horse coat designation
3 Fruit pastry
4 Sham locks
5 We inspire it
6 Either "New York Minute" co-star
7 TV comic Roseanne
8 Shawkat of "Arrested Development"
9 Some ThinkPads, e.g.
10 Like Albee's "The Sandbox"
11 Forerunner of 116-Down
12 Moves forward
13 Chief
14 "Jeopardy!" maven Jennings
15 Throws in
16 Tire trouble
17 In an aimless way
19 Some are self-guided
23 Cancel out
24 Clef type
28 Aerodynamic car style
31 Legendary Spanish hero
33 2006 Olympics host, to locals
34 Princess costume item
35 Santa's hands
37 Canon camera model
38 Arles article
39 Palindromic Nabokov title
40 Synagogue scroll
41 Texan dish, a.k.a. "bowl of red"
42 "I've — up to here!"
43 Thug's knife
45 Ten C-notes
49 Rush hour pace
50 Biblical peak
51 Montana birthplace of Evel Knievel
55 Casual day cry
58 Mineo of "Exodus"
60 Made a choice
61 Debtors' letters
62 Abbr. on a bounced check
63 Famed fable writer
64 Beat for James Levine
65 Core of an Apple
67 Butlers and such
70 1/1760 mile units
71 Hoopster nicknamed "the Diesel"
72 Bring together
73 Canonized French woman
74 Take risks
76 Comedian Fields
77 Market analyst's concern
78 Bygone time
82 Whom cops collar
85 Sandra or Ruby
86 Licorice-flavored liqueur
87 Massachusetts cape
88 Put into service
89 Sprees
90 New Jersey's state tree
93 Distant
96 Scholastic show-off
97 — Square (flagship Macy's site)
99 Western New York prison
100 Schlock
103 Many Mideasterners
104 Wild guess
105 Corn — (Southern bread)
106 Love, to Virgil
109 High tea, e.g.
110 Wee and weak
112 Forage storage site
113 Geraint's wife, in Arthurian legend
114 They outrank pvts.
116 Plame affair org.
117 Slimy stuff
118 Jeans brand

Wherever You Go

Across

1 Like some backed-up data
7 Chimps' kin in 20-Across
13 Sun-blocking event
20 Island east of Sumatra
21 Deal-killing phrase
22 Font first called Messenger
23 Meaning of SMH, in texting
25 Jersey city near Jersey City
26 Responses to pain
27 The things here
28 Church keys, at times
30 Spelling in acting
32 Knotty wood
33 Formerly, formerly
34 German chancellor Merkel
37 Princess-costume item
40 Traction aid
44 With 108-Across, Attica, Sing Sing, etc.
46 Bruins legend Bobby
47 Sound at a shearing
50 Suffix with Benedict
51 Hit the hay
52 Windfall, so to speak
55 Considers (to be)
58 Meadow
59 Rap-sheet listings
61 Large cross
62 Actress Meryl and siblings
64 Honking birds
65 Ill-fated flier of myth
67 "Father of the Blues"
70 Family of Dutch-French painters
72 Rum-based highball
75 Emanations of mystique
77 Time-saving kind of shopping
81 Infamous Ugandan
82 Exchanges
84 Penn Plaza arena
86 Vikings' language
87 Thermal winter wear
89 Either of two Equator parallels
92 Quick-wink link
93 Brunch fish
94 Fair-hiring abbr.
95 Group advising Britain's monarch
98 How stocks may be sold
100 Reduces to bits, as potatoes
101 Quartz varieties
102 Frenzied way to run
105 Engendered
107 German industrial valley
108 See 44-Across
112 Characteristic
115 Cheerleader's shout
118 Tufted ___ (small songbirds)
119 HBO hit series, or another title for this puzzle
123 Makes possible
124 List of meeting matters
125 Forth
126 Inserts new bullets
127 Eta, het, or aitch
128 Many Bob Marley fans

Down

1 Docs at deliveries
2 Bowery neighbor in NYC
3 Depict, in a way
4 Longtime LPGA player Juli
5 Twice tre
6 Shrink
7 Tab-grabber's words
8 Orbison and Rogers
9 ESPN's Arthur ___ Courage Award
10 "Forget it!", in Inverness
11 Like much of Antarctica
12 Coupe alternative
13 Sound comeback
14 Pen that has layers?
15 Job for a grease monkey
16 Pressed
17 Tightwad
18 Clairvoyants
19 Surrealist painter Max
24 Three on a phone's 4
29 Angler's entangler
31 Cry at the World Cup
32 Strut like a steed
34 Low-pH substances
35 Trio of trios
36 Feminist Germaine
37 Lose energy
38 Inner Hebrides isle
39 "Wheel of Fortune" buy
41 Mechanical learning style
42 Gradual wearing away
43 "Woof!"
45 Oklahoma city
47 Churlish sort
48 Baseball's Moisés or Jesús
49 Chimes in
52 Galileo's birthplace
53 Prophetic sign
54 Ella, first woman elected governor
56 Making kitten sounds
57 Sunnis, say
60 Amps (up)
63 Occasion for PR pics
64 "Did ___ and gimble in the wabe" ("Jabberwocky")
66 Director Ethan or Joel
68 Tandoor-baked flatbread
69 Bombs that bomb
71 System of reasoning
72 Shopping Shangri-la
73 Melville's "Typee" sequel
74 Bad-luck bringer
76 Pippi Longstocking creator Lindgren
78 Land parcel
79 Davis who wed Ruby Dee
80 Resounding rings
83 Perlman of "Cheers"
84 Stir emotionally
85 1974 CIA film-spoof
88 Airbus, e.g.
90 Rock singer Ocasek
91 Writing collaborator
95 Foreshadow
96 "Gross!"
97 Shrinks, in a sense
98 With hands on hips
99 Stat in MLB's Triple Crown
102 Après
103 Its state quarter has a lighthouse
104 In base 8
106 Kingly or queenly
107 Slowing, in music: abbr.
109 Oscar winner Kedrova
110 Bumped off
111 Mrs. Dick Tracy, née Trueheart
112 Mobile home?
113 Got a lift
114 Miles away
116 Med-sch. class
117 Zeus's wife
120 Fulfilled
121 Genetic-info carrier
122 Campus grp. of the '60s

Au Pairs

Across

1 Benefit
5 Bas-relief mixture
10 "Psst!" alternative
14 Oaf
18 Luxury-hotel chain
19 After today, to José
21 Spot for a nosh
22 Neofuturistic architect Saarinen
23 Sizes up some layouts?
25 Pickle type
26 Boris Godunov, e.g.
27 Initial stage
28 Domain
30 Paul of "Sideways"
32 They might be heard in a break room?
36 Slush Puppies' carbonated kin
37 Ace played by Jim Carrey
40 Duff
41 Suffix with hip
42 Freudian topic
43 Chemically nonreactive
47 Two in a quart, for short
48 Pub ___ (drinking events)
51 South American cowboy named for a Marx brother?
55 Pedicure focus
56 Leibovitz and Lennox
57 Mollify
58 Is off
59 Paleo- opposite
60 New Mexico art colony
62 Sass
63 Camel ___ (figure-skating move)
64 Home owner's payment: abbr.
65 Floppy tête topper
68 Grayish-brown bath item?
71 Exodus leader
72 Canned
73 Birdbrain
74 Hosp. caregiver
75 Earthly paradise
77 Frank McCourt memoir
78 Furniture giant from Sweden
79 Cause to swell
81 Anxious
85 Tabasco and Oaxaca, e.g.
87 Gorgeous woman's adorable ones?
89 Rubbernecks
90 Mex. Mrs.
91 Deck with a Wheel of Fortune card
92 Table scrap
93 Home to Jazz players
94 NYSE listing
96 Brought downward
99 Plumed wading bird
101 Nickname for a Hepburn, when she acted trashy?
105 Intensified suddenly
107 Kenmore brand owner
108 Big name in health insurance
112 Sari-clad royal
113 Lie alongside
115 This puzzle's word pairs show seven ways one may do it
118 One-named deco artist
119 Move, in Realtor lingo
120 Soul singer Nina
121 ___ Bator, Mongolia
122 Snafu
123 High-chair feature
124 Skewered dish from Asia
125 Cooped (up)

Down

1 Disco-dancer type
2 Mideast sultanate
3 Weighty responsibility
4 Assimilate mentally
5 MLB bosses
6 "The Raven" poet's inits.
7 Wolf (down)
8 Wise people
9 Hoopster dubbed "the Diesel"
10 Tack on
11 What acrophobics fear
12 Island in immigration history
13 Kunis of "Black Swan"
14 Whale, dolphin, or porpoise
15 With 67-Down, news anchor Holt desires owning eateries?
16 Deliver an address
17 Literature Nobelist Lessing
20 Get ___ on the wrist
24 Ides rebuke
29 WWII hero Audie
31 Bishops' headwear, in Britain
33 Operatic passage
34 Mammal's canine tooth
35 Cat, in Chihuahua
37 1970s Chevy
38 Jennifer with a 2011 fiction Pulitzer
39 "Cat", always, or "dog", sometimes
41 Contempt
44 Part of BCE
45 Furl
46 Bell-shaped bulb flower
49 Feudal figure
50 Blackthorn fruits
52 Made reference to
53 Fervor
54 Alpha star in Auriga (Lat.: "little goat")
55 Hogwash
58 Fuel-econ. rater
61 Oinkers' quarters
63 Vocal : cantata :: instrumental : ___
64 "Rouen Cathedral" painter
65 Caan's "Misery" co-star Kathy
66 Have a life
67 See 15-Down
69 Rx-writers' org.
70 Teapot part
71 Course list
73 Smidgen
76 Fictional No or Who
78 Think up
79 Uncle Sam and Yosemite Sam have them
80 Norse war god
82 Christian in fashion
83 "Pretty Woman" star Richard
84 Cornerstone abbr.
86 Carotids, e.g.
87 Something knit, mopped, or arched
88 Was a bear?
90 Shoulder blade
95 Readies for the OR
97 Withdraw gradually
98 Vessel for an ocular bath
99 Violinist Zimbalist
100 Harsh light
101 Potato, say
102 Toyota subcompact
103 Waffle House wafter
104 "Lead ___ into temptation …"
106 Flit
109 Prefix with marketing
110 Indian flatbread
111 It may rhyme with rant or font
114 Buzz Lightyear, for one
116 "Not ___ bet!"
117 Driver's 180°

Guys' Guise

Across
1 "Beats me!"
7 Per ___ (yearly)
12 Johnny Bench's benchmates
16 Toronto's prov.
19 Thumbs-up
20 "Queen of Mean" hotelier Helmsley
21 Vaccine type
22 Paleo- opposite
23 He's easy on the ears?
25 He's no peacenik?
27 Younger Obama daughter
28 Seeming eternity
29 Tiresome routines
31 Yiddish grandma
32 Atahualpa's people
34 Josh
36 It may keep a bay at bay
37 Sphere
40 He often needs treatment?
43 Lavishes affection (on)
44 Hardworking person
46 Zenith
47 Unvarying
49 Mallorca, por ejemplo
50 Pyrotechnic particles
53 Ricochet
55 Mineral-bath site
58 Still state
59 Part of HOMES
60 He's full of clichés?
62 Innately footless
64 Kohoutek, e.g.
66 Cast (off)
67 Equatorial African country
69 He's despicable?
72 Memory slip
73 Burton's "Becket" co-star
75 Crucifixes
76 Cinco or ocho
78 He's all wet and babbles?
80 Trillion: prefix
81 CNN's "___ Burnett OutFront"
84 Milano Mr.
85 Brewers Hall of Famer Robin
86 Construction beam
88 Hershey candy in a tube
89 Business partners, often
90 Italian port on the Adriatic
91 Concerns
93 SeaWorld orca show being phased out
96 He makes sense?
101 Two cents' worth
102 "Slaves of New York" author Janowitz
103 Like days of yore
104 Insignificant
106 Vote in
108 Really gross
109 Heave-ho
111 Nets and Nats, for two
115 He can hold his wine (and yours)?
117 He smells when he gets burned?
120 To the ___ degree
121 An orchestra tunes to one
122 Cardiac ventricles' neighbors
123 When deliveries are hopping?
124 "Get it?"
125 Refuse
126 Short-tempered
127 "Mamma Mia!" setting

Down
1 Copies cats
2 Workplace-protection org.
3 Egyptian fertility deity
4 Indian metropolis
5 Make better
6 Glance or loss lead-in
7 Very nearly
8 Type of tetra
9 Like T-Fal cookware
10 Prefix with form
11 Knotty craft
12 Way to be spoiled
13 Son of Aphrodite
14 Sire's counterpart in horse breeding
15 Thick slice
16 Even if dared for money
17 Tyro
18 Monopoly top hat, cat, etc.
24 Behind
26 Part of HOMES
30 Function
33 Risked being bleeped
35 O'Neill title trees
37 Ear-related
38 Sub ___ (secretly)
39 He's for smoking weed?
41 River with a U-turn in Bern
42 Guam, e.g.: abbr.
43 Tony-winning choreographer Agnes
45 Satirize
48 S'il ___ plait
51 Nappy wearer's buggy
52 Aircraft flap used in banking
53 Jazz singer Laine
54 Brought into agreement
55 He's holey?
56 Grunting group
57 Yearn
60 Brest buddies
61 Birds, when heading aloft
63 The Platters hit covered by Ringo
64 Emulate Emeril
65 Puzzling
67 Brahma and Vishnu, e.g.
68 Yours: Fr.
70 Haul of hot stuff
71 Without a doubt
74 Jet-black, poetically
77 Maid of "Merry Men" legend
79 Corrosive build-up
80 Subj. that uses sine language
82 Small intestine segments
83 Prone to prying
86 Powerful wind
87 What jailbirds are behind
89 Loud kiss
90 Inverse of lean muscle
92 Toy racer in a groove
93 They're aft, on seacraft
94 Rock salt
95 "Cocoon" Oscar winner Don
97 Its icing isn't kosher?
98 Antlered Yellowstone grazer
99 "No injuries here"
100 ___ Field (the "New Shea")
105 Brooklyn Dodgers' Pee Wee
107 Walked heavily
108 Desktop image
110 Handling the matter now
112 Pay for hands
113 Fraction of a min.
114 Dried and withered
116 Japan's Prime Minister Shinzo ___
118 GPS suggestion
119 Opp. of pos.

Film Splices

Across

1 Music staff sign
6 Responded in court
10 Emporium
14 Nightstand item
18 Slangy suffix in event ads
19 Part one plays
20 Mosque deity
21 "Che!" actor Sharif
22 Ms. Foster foils a hideout delivery by the Marx Brothers?
25 Kid-lit detective —— the Great
26 "The Ice Storm" director
27 An evil town illuminates Chaplin's antics?
29 "Definitely!"
30 "The Simpsons" son
33 Sushi bar tuna
34 Famed Van Gogh floral
35 Cold weather cupful
36 Soul: Fr.
37 Singer Turner
39 Inspector Clouseau injects Batman?
47 Dreary
48 "Hud" Oscar winner Patricia
49 Golf ball props
50 A Scot's "Afraid nots"
51 Israel's Abba
52 Solo at La Scala
54 Abbr. for A. Cuomo
55 Alabama city in 1965 news
56 Cap worn with a kilt
57 Ms. Heigl has a productive in-flight tryst with Mr. Clooney?
62 Tiny bit
63 Snakelike swimmer
64 Like many dorms
65 Mr. Caine is disguised as Ms. Thurman to get even?
72 Droop
75 Nobles above viscounts
76 Helpful connections
77 River of York
78 Ireland, to the Irish
79 Latin 101 verb
80 "—— is money"
82 Brewer's supply
84 Broadway backer
85 Mr. Powell solves the murder of O'Toole's lean Spaniard?
90 Sheriff of Mayberry
91 Toronto's prov.
92 "Affliction" actor Nick
93 Pull up stakes
97 Exec's appt.
98 Periphery
99 "I am so dense!"
102 A Pixar insect gets a Hitchcockian rescue?
107 Nook
109 "The Eternal City"
110 A frat is terrorized by a beehive-like place?
113 Tiger's ex-wife
114 Firmed at the gym
115 Jane Fonda, to Bridget
116 Bridge, Italian-style
117 Hollywood's Gus Van ——
118 Wraps, as in filming
119 Burro's outburst
120 Double curves

Down

1 Insured's medical bill share
2 Origami bird, often
3 Director Fritz and singer k.d.
4 Silents star Jannings
5 Subject of "The Social Network"
6 Debate side
7 Eton john
8 Shade trees
9 He loved Lucy
10 Eleventh-century year Macbeth died
11 Landed
12 Risqué
13 Some golf course names
14 Sound in "nice," but not "Nice"
15 Asian nannies
16 Unshiny finish
17 Phone menu imperative
20 Like a fighting cat's back
23 Flinch or wince, e.g.
24 Glossy kind of paint
28 Persian Gulf country
31 Monarch in a palais
32 Vintner's type of acid
35 Martial artist Jackie
36 "Just as I thought!"
37 The fountain in 109-Across
38 Singer Turner
39 "Fantastic Four" actress Jessica
40 Line from a Singer
41 Wood used for decks
42 Resting on
43 "—— a vacation!"
44 Lavish fete
45 Prefix with sphere
46 Ivan the Terrible, e.g.
47 Put in some chips
52 Put in some chips
53 Word with rage or runner
54 Shore bird
55 Author Silverstein
57 Big name in headphones
58 Comic strip shrieks
59 Agnus —— (Lamb of God)
60 Maritime spinoff of "JAG"
61 Lacquered metalware
62 Dot on a map, maybe
65 Insect repellent ingredient
66 Some baby bumps?
67 Scottish Gaelic
68 "Lassie" boy
69 Draft status
70 Laze about
71 Lighter fuel
72 Exhalation of regret
73 Specialty
74 Toothpaste option
78 Suffix with defer or differ
80 Rust-resistant sheet metal
81 The Hoosiers state: abbr.
82 Genghis Khan, e.g.
83 Sternward
84 Gnu, gazelle, or impala
86 Their acting isn't kosher?
87 "Pretty nice!"
88 Chic, in the '60s
89 Aquarium buildup
93 Has the nerve
94 "The Hot Zone" virus
95 Spice in curries and chili
96 Go-between
97 Internet —— (cultural ideas)
99 "Concentration" host Hugh
100 Egg-shaped
101 Evil spells
103 Wise to
104 Discover
105 Pequod captain
106 It may be self-guided
108 Corp. money managers
111 Spanish "a"
112 Shoat shelter

A Separate Piece

Across

1 Rapper's bandana, perhaps
6 Cause of shaking
10 Sylvester, Jane's "Glee" role
13 Admit
18 Sunset Strip disco, the Whisky —
19 First-rate
20 Tries to tan
21 Idolize
22 "It's not an "it"; she's female!"?
25 Archie Bunker type
26 Ball participant
27 Beyond portly
28 Strong, as potables
29 Possible result of recycling plate glass?
33 — Aviv
34 List-ending abbr.
37 Allan- — (Robin Hood cohort)
38 Author Anya or saint Elizabeth
39 Expose
40 Sourpuss
42 Units of some sentences
45 Flak
47 Truth about the guy who golfs?
52 Secured at the pier
55 Gold-medal skater Baiul
56 Pre-1917 ruler
57 Island partner of Principe
58 Pitched in
62 "The Colossus" poet Sylvia
64 Most of Turkey's in it
65 Six-pack muscles
68 Warmly greet what one surfs on?
72 Norm: abbr.
73 Past the curfew
75 Greek column style
76 "Meet the Fockers", e.g.
78 Staple of Hawaiian music
81 Twice tetra-
83 Expels, as an ATM card
87 Sacred Saudi city
88 "This Boggle set is really big!"?
92 "Hey, bro!"
95 Holdup
96 Minuscule
97 Tiff
99 "I wonder who's knocking" response
102 Fourth estate
105 Put the kibosh on
106 Sphere
107 "Are we watching boxing here?"?
111 Chuck of martial arts movies
113 Value system
114 "Death of a Salesman" family
117 Steer clear of
118 Request to shipbuilders?
122 Give a ribbing
123 Secluded valley
124 Camaro classic, — -Z
125 Welsh "dwarf dog"
126 European viper
127 Soul singer Cooke
128 E-reader brand
129 Four-door, often

Down

1 Perp prosecutors
2 Prayer-opening words
3 Alitalia hub
4 Broker
5 "Ha-ha, ya fell for it!"
6 Golf course components
7 Seeming eternity
8 "Hulk" director Lee
9 Lay new turf
10 From Geneve or Gruyeres
11 Ousts from office
12 Serpentine shape
13 Toil
14 Menu bar word
15 Why the chicken visited the church gift shop on the other side of the road?
16 Wrinkle remover?
17 Plant whose hairs sting
20 Seaducks akin to mergansers
23 Take seriously
24 Blood-typing letters
28 Canal locale
30 Small intestine segments
31 Close
32 Write (down) quickly
34 Boomeranging ringing, say
35 Taxing journey
36 Upper limits
39 Regional wildlife
41 Dullsville
43 Deteriorate
44 Thought to be guilty
46 Overly
48 Over again
49 Where Bill and Hillary met
50 Simba's mate
51 Olive — (army uniforms)
53 Radiate
54 Part of 93-Across
57 Former hoopster "The Diesel"
59 Barre room bend
60 Writer Umberto
61 "— disturb"
63 Kiddie's "piggy"
65 Coll. endowment source
66 Oven control setting
67 Scrutinize some dame?
69 "The Mitten State": abbr.
70 Regrets
71 — vu
74 Marner's creator
77 Hit the road
79 Close
80 Comedians go for them
82 Time of one's life?
84 Mint product
85 Actress Collette
86 Hades river
89 Obstacles for Hannibal
90 "Side Effects" star Rooney
91 Part of some athletes' face paint
93 Beyond aid at the ER
94 Pip's love in "Great Expectations"
97 Many a Beethoven work
98 Verified beyond doubt
100 High regard
101 Wharton's Frome
103 Any minute
104 Some have toxic leaves
107 More expansive
108 Informal greetings
109 Trap during an Arctic storm, say
110 SUV named for a lake
112 Bailiff's command
115 Geeky sort
116 Long story
118 Some film ratings
119 Debate side
120 Where Brits go?
121 Cacophony

Extra Syllable, Puh-lease

Across

1 Month after Shevat
5 Stays fresh
10 Steakhouse specification
14 Exam for H.S. juniors
18 Zero
19 Initial occurrence
20 Empire State canal
21 Former host of Dr. Phil
23 Sitcom about a pair with highly ornate style?
26 Ethnic group
27 Slammer dweller
28 Aviation hazard
29 Soap operas, e.g.
31 Scented-chemical assault à la "Star Wars"?
37 "Roots" author Alex
39 Luxury-hotel-chain name
40 Toy-truck brand
41 Brest buddies
42 Chowder type
43 Filmed
45 Milan opera house La —
50 School of tomorrow?
51 "Walden" author after his bath, say?
55 Typographical goof
57 Calligrapher's need
58 So last year
59 Gather in
60 Jay-Z's genre
61 Pressure to get hitched?
64 Thailand neighbor
66 Greek X
68 Salon supply
69 Fabricate
70 What happens when Homer Simpson's pious neighbor strays?
75 Part of R.S.V.P.
76 Prefix meaning "height"
77 Fashion designer Anna
78 Rite words
79 Greatly value
84 Catty remark about Mother Earth's downfall?
88 Peace, to Pliny
89 Macho dudes
90 Give the boot
91 Hunter's garb, for short
92 Sup
93 Comic actor Murphy
96 Prefix with sphere
97 Is flexible
98 Former TV series featuring athletic bras and jockstraps?
105 "Anne of Green Gables" setting
106 Biological pouch
107 Allow
110 "Divine Comedy" poet
111 "Get those big oafs moving!"?
117 Nine: prefix
118 Forearm bone
119 Ordeal
120 Furniture giant from Sweden
121 Feudal laborer
122 Bottom-heavy fruit
123 Uppity sorts
124 Yukon or Northwest: abbr.

Down

1 Not for
2 Duvet filler
3 Deviations
4 Cash-back incentives
5 "M*A*S*H" setting
6 Grammy-winning producer Brian
7 Abbr. for a lawyer
8 Little: Fr.
9 Graf of tennis
10 Ponder, as evidence
11 Miss the mark
12 Small, in Dogpatch
13 Instructional unit
14 Braised-beef entrée
15 Parsley piece
16 Suffix with sect
17 Place-setting setting
22 Pianist Dame Myra
24 Abbr. for a lawyer
25 Came down with
30 Moose relative
32 Analogy punctuation mark
33 Rival of Target
34 "This round's —"
35 James Bond's alma mater
36 Soft and fluffy
37 Damage
38 Marceau's "mine"
42 Dip holder
43 Sought damages
44 Posterior, as paws
46 Livestock enclosures
47 Beatles song "Eight Days —"
48 Rent
49 Where it's always peak season?
51 Totally wreck
52 Mimic
53 Gargantuan
54 JFK takeoff listing
56 Pop the question
61 Finish in front
62 Proofs of DOB, e.g.
63 Inuit boat similar to a kayak
64 Madre's milk
65 To the point, in legal Latin
66 Whodunit hint
67 Product for frizzy locks
70 "Parsley is gharsley" poet
71 Essay conclusion?
72 "Buenos —"
73 Cut and paste, say
74 Former Yankee Guidry
75 Dry, like some vino
79 Hobo
80 Swab again
81 1978 Cheech and Chong stoner film
82 "The Fountainhead" author Ayn
83 Former mates
85 Turn over — (improve oneself)
86 Wished undone
87 Grp. promoting sobriety since 1874
92 Home to Lions and Tigers
94 Fawn's mom
95 Draft, as a contract
96 Broad, knotted neck pieces
97 Belgian songwriter Jacques
98 Cross the kiddie pool
99 Turgenev and Pavlov
100 "No man is an island" poet
101 Computer key
102 Schindler with a list
103 Wray of "King Kong"
104 Gems mostly from Australia
108 Latin road
109 Romanov ruler
112 Bullring "Bravo!"
113 Genetic-info carrier
114 Coffee-hour vessel
115 Carnival city, briefly
116 Shoot the breeze

Heard Mentality

Across

1 Buffalo hockey player
6 Weird
9 Taj Mahal site
13 Money-back offer
19 Martian, say
20 Word with Blu or X
21 Clamorous
22 "24" actress Cuthbert
23 007, wasted and looking old?
26 Lynn, to Vanessa
27 Stow cargo
28 Video game pioneer
29 Believer in a hands-off God
31 What jailbirds do that "flies"
32 Colorado ski town
34 Part of a Reuben after overgrilling?
37 Skeletons in the closet
40 "The Andy Griffith Show" boy
41 Rail-riding drifter
42 Mistreatment
43 Declares firmly
44 BBs and such
45 Ovine whine
48 Carved pumpkins are in this?
51 Cowbell sound emitted by a cow?
53 Put the kibosh on
54 Goofed
55 Prefix with practice
56 Hauntingly strange
57 Tin Man : heart :: Scarecrow : ——
58 Chess piece
60 Cuts out surgically
62 —— Paulo, Brazil
64 Inherently virtuous?
67 Govt. mortgage grp.
68 Lasts
70 Nutty
71 Alternative to Adidas or Nike
73 "SNL" producer Michaels
74 Young fellow
75 1950s series, "The —— Kid"
76 "Exodus" hero played by Paul
79 Like a smile on one's face, often?
82 Raised on pasta, polenta, and pizza?
85 Suffix with alcohol
86 Russian river and range
87 Small inlets
88 Deadly
89 Prune or crop
90 Getting —— years
91 Sunday-drive vista
93 Package-wrapping policy of the post office?
98 Fragment, as of pottery
99 Target of an uppercut
100 Cruise stopovers
101 Manatees' milieu
103 Queens stadium surname
107 Territory
109 LightHouse beneficiaries expressed relief?
112 Greek goddess of wisdom
113 Sty cry
114 "The Waste Land" poet's monogram
115 Farm equipment company
116 Do security duty
117 Bygone fliers to JFK
118 Verbal thumbs-up
119 Append

Down

1 Wry comedian Mort
2 Actress Shawkat
3 Nickname for the Mavs' home
4 Practice for a performance
5 Humanities subj.
6 Pontificates
7 Israeli war hero Moshe
8 Beautician, at times
9 Priest's vestment
10 Sweet treats
11 Ancient markings
12 —— Ababa, Ethiopia
13 Long-term care facility
14 Roth of "Inglourious Basterds"
15 Café
16 Up and doing
17 Unifying idea
18 Lop- —— (rabbit type)
24 Deeply engrossed
25 Get rid of
30 Dolt
33 Sowing implement
35 Like some terriers' coats
36 Dwellings
37 Herb in stuffing
38 Black, poetically
39 Morsel for Miss Muffet
40 "Metamorphoses" poet
43 Revise, as the Constitution
44 ISP spun off Time Warner
45 Canoe material source, historically
46 Writer Diamant or Desai
47 Mighty long time
49 Body structure
50 Met solos
51 Kind of shark
52 Coral compositions
55 Hardness-scale creator
57 Tied up
58 Map line, maybe
59 O'er and o'er again
60 Martini & —— vermouth
61 Author Jong
62 Flaky blankets
63 To the point, in law
65 AuctionWeb, today
66 Performs perfectly
68 "The Time Machine" race
69 Homecoming, e.g.
72 Bestow
74 Texter's chortle
75 Normandy city
76 Prado collection
77 Caboose
78 In an aimless way
80 Creatively fresh
81 Doorway sides
82 Skye of "Say Anything"
83 Small-screen heartthrob
84 Applied a sterile dressing, e.g.
87 Give approval
89 More petite
91 Nuances
92 Some recyclables
93 Toss out
94 Eighth Greek letter
95 Correct
96 Choral group section
97 Classic fruity sodas
98 Have a feeling
102 Queens's Long Island ——
104 Cast off
105 Horizontal kin of a Dagwood
106 Temptation location
108 Yoko from Tokyo
110 Bible divisions: abbr.
111 Muckraker Tarbell

Pun-itive Diet

Across

1 Lifesaver sandwich?
5 Hold with a vise
10 Cognizant
15 Prefix with medic or legal
19 Very much
20 TV-signal component
21 Seuss's ecofriendly creature, the ——
22 Latin 101 verb
23 Start of an original verse
27 Flowerlike decoration
28 Accelerates
29 "A house —— a home"
30 Evening, in Torino
32 Whichever
33 Some cordillera dwellers
35 Henna or madder-root product
39 Avian perch
42 "Dirt"-pudding cookie
43 "Garfield" canine
44 Line 2 of the verse
51 Cash drawers
53 Frost and Burns
54 Pet-food brand
55 True
56 Chopper's landing platform
58 McEntire of country
59 Spanish "Cheers!"
60 Oratorio solo
61 Entice
64 "Titanic" theme singer Dion
65 Suffix with auction
68 With 89-Across, Line 3 of the verse
71 Civic or Fit
72 Muck
74 Babbles
75 The whole nine yards
77 Fey and Turner
78 Begin the bidding
79 Stuffs oneself
83 Cries of discovery
84 Rare bills
85 Fifties series, "The —— Kid"
88 Sitcom housemate of Kate
89 See 68-Across
93 Potentially disastrous
94 Descriptor of Silver's rider
95 "Skyfall" singer
96 Died down
98 Narrow waterways
102 Part of TGIF: abbr.
103 Scarlett's home
105 Brazil metropolis, São ——
106 Gilda who played Litella, Wawa, etc.
109 Joint-twisting injuries
114 End of the verse
118 Modern pentathlon weapon
119 City near Düsseldorf
120 Last Oldsmobile produced
121 Wander about
122 Bonny gal
123 Feats
124 Strung along
125 Common bills

Down

1 "Good Morning Starshine" musical
2 Often-pesky boy in "Blondie"
3 Some retinal receptors
4 Missouri River tribe
5 Hiker's water flask
6 German pistol
7 Nabokov novel
8 Feel nostalgia for
9 Ceremonial grandeur
10 Not overcooked, as pasta
11 "Cheers" actor Harrelson
12 Curved paths
13 Double-crosser
14 Prefix with skeleton
15 Old hat
16 Brand under Whirlpool
17 Silky synthetic
18 Admin. helpers
24 Teensy
25 Brewers' and bakers' supplies
26 Done with
31 Specialized lingo
33 Wine's bouquet, say
34 It's broken by anchors
35 Type of IRA
36 Emmy-winning Falco
37 Pickle herb
38 "You've Got Mail" screenwriter Ephron
40 Corrida shout
41 Umpire's call
42 How some dares are done
45 Forest's co-star in "Lee Daniels' the Butler"
46 Sibling's daughters
47 Vaccine type
48 Archaeological find
49 Hawaii's Kea or Loa
50 Respected tribe member
52 Small shoots
57 River to the Seine
58 Contraption cartoonist Goldberg
59 Málaga madame
61 Least iffy
62 Verve
63 EPA-banned pesticide
64 Quote from
65 Cornerstone abbr.
66 Nobelist statesman Root
67 Charge toward
69 Go up against
70 Utter chaos
73 Sprinting event
76 F. Scott Fitzgerald's wife
78 Olympian Jesse
79 Madrigal group, maybe
80 Came to rest
81 Grow weary
82 Future fuchsia
84 Harness-race pace
85 Relinquishing, as territory
86 Treatment for swelling
87 "Erie Canal" song mule
90 Creator of Bede and Marner
91 Congeals
92 Whaling weapon
97 Where one might have a cow?
98 Pitch meant to persuade
99 Florida's "Cigar City"
100 Ancient markings
101 Healing succulents
102 Destined
104 Houston ballplayer
106 Greet the day
107 Israeli airline
108 Govern
110 'Do worn by Hendrix
111 Monopoly token retired in 2013
112 "Scream" actress Campbell
113 Understands
115 Proof-ending Latin letters
116 Put to work
117 Newsman Koppel

A Game of Motto

Across

1 Catnip, e.g.
5 Chapters of history
9 Skater —— Anton Ohno
14 Babushka
19 Polo crossed it
20 Riot-control spray
21 Farm machine used on hay
22 Arctic or Antarctic
23 Chutzpah as well as hot air?
26 "Dallas" matriarch
27 Omani sovereign
28 Wingtip's tip
29 Meaning of "rhino-"
30 Biathlon weapon
31 Hot-cross-bun crosser, e.g.
33 Lot in life
35 Transmission-repair chain with "beep-beep" ads
37 Backwoods treat?
43 Color on political maps
46 "Payment later" note
47 Tax prep VIP
48 NFL Network anchor Rich
49 Fanning in films
52 Southerners carrying a certain bread?
56 Manhattan East Side's —— Drive
58 It's toxic
59 Word with rate or ribs
60 French fashion monogram
61 What a game may end in
62 Utopian settings
63 More like doilies
65 "That hurts!"
68 Raises
70 CBS symbol
71 Group of portable toilets?
75 Foot: Lat.
78 Yippie Hoffman
79 "New Look" couturier
80 League of Nations home
82 Regional flora and fauna
85 Prefix meaning within
87 Certain gametes
90 Flat-rental sign
91 Heath's "Brokeback Mountain" role
92 B&O stop
93 Chimp expert with a joke-response surname?
96 First name in soul
98 Bury
100 Part of USNA: abbr.
101 GPS heading
102 NFL "zebra"
103 Ump's ruling on a pitch, perhaps?
108 Pizza topping
111 Way off
112 Empire State canal
113 New England catch
115 Adherents
118 No big sleep
120 Exemplars of slowness
124 Midwest hub
125 "You're demanding quite some sound!"?
128 TV mother of Pebbles
129 Event with broncs and cheers
130 Depression-era migrant
131 Bone under one's watch
132 Rooms in la casa
133 Purse or cup, e.g.
134 Gym count
135 Pod veggies

Down

1 Witchy women
2 Jacob's womb mate
3 Small stream
4 Sea-named Monopoly avenue
5 High repute
6 Double-crosser
7 Sechs, sieben, ——, neun, . . .
8 Detonate
9 Bart Simpson's grandpa
10 Plains tribe
11 Miscellany
12 Eyeglasses "glass"
13 Harsh trial
14 Certain gamete
15 Baby bummer
16 With 84-Down, the Three Musketeers' motto and a hint to the puzzle's theme
17 Transportation option
18 Unrestricted
24 Rice : Houston :: Baylor : ——
25 Source of warmth
32 Make good on
34 Out of —— world
36 Kick in
37 Hit the sauce
38 "Yippee!"
39 Carol's "Mama's Family" character
40 Hydrodynamic duo
41 Loom thread crossing the warp
42 A Gandhi
44 James Bond's alma mater
45 Spillway sites
50 Put off by
51 Sneakers since 1916
53 Brit. record label
54 Keg party
55 "The Time Machine" race
57 Stagger
61 "Got it!", à la Mr. Moto
64 Mug, say
66 Edit menu "Go back"
67 Hi-tech visual effects: abbr.
69 H.S. math course
72 They're made up
73 Soup legume
74 1982 Disney sci-fi film
75 House Speaker before Boehner
76 Nevertheless
77 Glossy fabric
78 "Look —— this way . . ."
81 A move to approve
82 Put up with
83 "As to," on a memo
84 See 16-Down
86 Pioneer Boone, informally
88 —— diagram (set theory visual)
89 Banded quartz variety
93 Bridges of "The Big Lebowski"
94 Occult matters
95 Supervises
97 Blood-typing letters
99 Kitchen slot machine?
104 "Peer Gynt Suite" dancer
105 Cicero, notably
106 Little hombre
107 Shred
109 Marilyn's birth name
110 Brainstorming precipitates
113 Females who root
114 Pet with herbal "fur"
116 Manifest
117 "I did it!"
119 Nudge on Facebook
121 Not working
122 "Alias" actress Olin
123 Mmes., in Málaga
126 Lawn base
127 Tuck's partner

41

Think in Initials

Across

1 Jaunty
5 Juicy, as turkey meat
10 Sick as ——
14 "Li'l Abner" cartoonist Al
18 Region
19 "Cocoon" Oscar winner Don
21 Sundial numeral
22 Wahine's dance
23 Dietary supplement you pay for when it arrives?
25 Career slogan of an upbeat computer pro?
27 German city on the Ruhr
28 Paperboys, in a 1992 film title
30 Brings about
31 Jeanne d'Arc, e.g.: abbr.
33 Popeye's ward —— 'Pea
34 Browns at the beach
35 Book-to-film biopic about a sleuth for hire?
40 Just a lot of inanity in the surgery suite?
46 "Entourage" agent Gold
47 Not smooth, as gravy
49 Nights before holidays
50 Sound portion
51 Surrealist contemporary of Miró
53 Wings, to biologists
54 Oldest Cartwright son on "Bonanza"
55 Marzipan ingredient
56 One spotting NY's I-495 en route to the Hamptons, say?
59 Bird with crazy calls
61 "Sad to say"
62 The ones here: Sp.
63 City of "La Dolce Vita"
65 Exempli gratia, e.g.
67 —— Moines, Iowa
68 Comic about a fingerprinting genius?
73 Mischievous youngster
76 Letter before iota
77 Actress Falco
78 Golfer Els
80 Renown
83 Canasta objective
85 The Crusades but not the Punic Wars, e.g.?
89 Reparations
91 Thirteen popes
93 Commercial-designers' award
94 Camembert alternative
95 Like the Vikings
96 "Brian's Song" star James ——
97 Pesto, for one
98 Qty.
99 Relieve TV's Dr. Quincy or Robbins?
102 Absent Italian parent's musical title?
105 Cheerios-flavored
106 Home to Iowa State
108 Mineo of "Exodus"
109 Outlay
113 Worst, in a race
116 Retro photo tone
120 Reason a digital display might not work?
122 Blessing for clothes too tattered to save?
124 Burl on a tree
125 School founded by Henry VI
126 Crosses the threshold
127 Arduous journey
128 Unwelcome freshness
129 Cameo, maybe
130 University of Florida athlete
131 Figure (out), slangily

Down

1 Tempo
2 Greek deity of desire
3 Malbec, Medoc, etc.
4 "A Writer's Life" writer, Gay ——
5 Dallas hoopster, briefly
6 Portentous sign
7 "Able was —— …" (palindrome start)
8 Flat-bottomed boats
9 "Right ——" (usher's phrase)
10 Hertz competitor
11 Lit just a bit
12 Grease monkeys' containers
13 "Buon ——" ("Good day": It.)
14 Herbal "pet"
15 Pippa Middleton, to Prince George
16 Bending ballet move
17 Butter servings
20 Senior Saarinen in architecture
24 Keen about
26 —— virgins (ancient priestesses)
29 Fished for congers
32 Key of Beethoven's "Eroica"
34 Vibrato's volume-varying kin
35 Did a soup-kitchen task
36 Poker declaration words
37 Entrees of sole
38 Whine
39 Apple desktop since 1998
41 Ford-logo shape
42 Earthling
43 Worshipped one
44 One of Columbus's ship trio
45 Worshipped ones
48 Lab-dish inventor
52 Nuptial agreement
54 Warship fleets
55 Against
57 O.T. book read at Purim
58 Exude
60 Clumsy clod
64 Desertlike
66 Cerebral spark
69 Edges often hand-sewn
70 Summer, to Yves
71 Australian marsupial
72 Longtime record label
73 James ——, singer (with Ronstadt) of "Somewhere Out There"
74 Small fingers, in anatomy
75 Pre-euro Spanish coin
76 On edge
79 Josh
80 Venom-injecting tooth
81 French possessive
82 Griffin in game-show history
84 Salutation starter
86 Grad
87 Flaky, heat-resistant mineral
88 Works by Whittier and Whitman
90 Exorcism targets
92 7'1" retired basketball center
96 Wait on hand and foot
97 Depicting in a biased way
100 Spring movable feast
101 Love, in Lido
103 1962 novelty hit song "Monster ——"
104 Tips off
107 Nasal dividers
109 "Benevolent" lodge members
110 Former TV warrior princess
111 Handheld organizers: abbr.
112 What walls have, idiomatically
113 New Year song ender
114 Proofer's "Undo that dele"
115 Annual Pamplona runner
117 Machu Picchu's land
118 Foreboding time for Caesar
119 Sets a price of
121 Internet co. that owns Moviefone
123 Lith. or Lat., formerly

Part Latin

Across

1 Like clocks with hands
7 Diadem relative
12 Cuts off
18 Et —— (and the others, literally)
19 Marked down
21 Suffragist Bloomer
22 1983 film about a sizable wine bottle on ice?
24 American horse breed
25 Facilitate
26 1954–77 defense grp.
27 Skyrockets
29 Smoothness exemplar
30 Pass along
33 Smart path for food delivery?
36 Ancient Roman magistrate: var.
38 Debussy's "La ——"
39 Nashville-to-NYC dir.
40 Chilean chum
43 Levine of Maroon 5
47 Florida's Senator Rubio
52 The Jungfrau's range
55 Retail purveyor of music for the tub?
60 Faun, in part
61 Take hold
62 Home made of hides
63 Detox candidate
64 Had title to
66 TV producer Michaels
68 Diapers, in Derbyshire
70 Mrs. Chaplin, nee O'Neill
72 Holy one's excuse in a TV medical drama?
76 Use a Kindle or Nook
77 Dessert in a tall glass
80 Picket-line crossers
82 NASA outfit
85 Muslim worship leader
86 Twerp
90 Razor and coffeemaker brand
92 Present
93 Market's surveillance device?
96 Latin bones
97 No longer fresh
98 Cloak for Claudius
99 Big name at SeaWorld
101 Prefix with tonic
104 Zilch
107 Highlands girls
111 Masquerade as a smiling cartoon cat, in a song?
120 Lewd dude
121 Elitist
122 Key of Beethoven's Fourth
123 Taking too many meds
125 "Just as I thought!"
126 Of a heart chamber
128 Autobiography featuring an evil body part?
132 "—— Latin Lupe Lu" (1963 song)
133 Designed for one
134 Coop up
135 Neatnik's nightmares
136 "Kinky Boots" won six in 2013
137 Brought up

Down

1 More sore
2 Record player's stylus
3 Bread box?
4 Meadow
5 NOW and WHO, e.g.
6 Thief, Yiddish-style
7 Hand drum
8 Wages and interest
9 Blonde shade
10 Mrs. Gorbachev
11 "It's —— nothing"
12 Biblical strongman
13 Alt-rock genre
14 Ogden Nash specialty
15 Hall of Fame hoopster Baylor
16 Iranian money
17 Decaf-instant-coffee brand
20 Westerns actor Jack
22 Diamond protector
23 Bygone Egypt-Syr. alliance
28 Numbered hwy.
31 Herb Alpert sample from a former TV diner-owner?
32 —— Kippur
34 Humorist Lebowitz
35 Note from the CEO, maybe
37 Barbecue entrée
41 Iona College athlete
42 Four Holy Roman emperors
44 Pesticide banned by the EPA
45 Beame, NYC mayor before Ed
46 Unruly 'do
48 Ibsen play which could be subtitled "Cocoon"?
49 Leftover substances
50 Aboriginal Canadian tribe
51 Scull propellers
52 Back in time
53 Like an ebb tide
54 Far-reaching view
56 "Java" trumpeter Al
57 Faris of TV's "Mom"
58 Room for unwinding
59 Wine-label datum
65 Modern form of I.D.
67 Lines through Chicago's Loop
69 Coatrack projection
71 Elton John–Tim Rice musical
73 Long-range weapon: abbr.
74 Unadorned
75 Construction beams
77 Snaps or flicks
78 Latin I conjugation word
79 Tango complement
81 "—— is life"
83 E-file recipient
84 Tazo or Tetley product
87 Young newt
88 Writer Umberto
89 Mire
91 "Hud" Oscar winner Patricia
94 Jockey's "brake"
95 Cat with a tailless variety
100 Prefix meaning "bad"
102 Pricey furs
103 Awry
105 "I wish!"
106 Common door sign
108 Human puppet
109 Reverberated
110 Whiskey serving
111 Biblical hymn
112 Release from lashings
113 Civil wrongs
114 Bios rarely seen by their subjects
115 Trees hard-hit by a disease
116 —— on the line
117 "—— skin off my nose"
118 Start of Cookie Monster's song
119 Computer key
124 Wilder who played Wonka
127 Pub quaff
129 Engine starter: abbr.
130 Color-TV pioneer
131 Way off

Vowel Swaps

Across

1 Down's thickness
5 Longed
10 Apples on some desks
14 Writer Martin or Kingsley
18 Cornhusker State city
20 Museum docent, often
21 Way to sit by
22 "Critique of Pure Reason" author
23 Game of refusing to release your IRS returns?
25 Palindromic time
26 Get the kitty going
27 On edge
28 Paddywagon?
31 "Mazel __!"
32 Caesar with two Emmys
33 "I could __ horse!"
35 Demolished
36 Lerner's "Camelot" collaborator
38 Queue after Q
39 St. Louis landmark
41 Be in a bee, maybe
43 Holiday reef material?
49 Wildly popular
52 Keanu of "Constantine"
53 Eponymous Belgian town with springs
54 Life, to Luigi
56 Vaccine fluids
57 Made calls from home?
58 "Told you so!"
59 Rubinstein in cosmetics history
61 The Eiger, e.g.
62 Impel
63 Halloween-edition mints?
66 Alkali in cleansers
67 "Enough!", in Napoli
69 Paving goo
70 Strike back, e.g.
72 Small, writ small
74 Dog rolling on the rug, trying for treats?
79 Prefix with stat
82 Infamous Amin
83 Where Turin's Torino
84 Malarkey
85 EE, on a shoe box
86 Make fun of
88 Lyft alternative
89 Junior whopper?
90 Chevy muscle car
91 Flaxen-haired
93 Features of a past Hollywood prima donna?
97 Lavish spread
99 Coop group
100 Ottoman Empire title
101 Preferences
103 Barfly's perch
106 Part of CPU
107 A bursa is one
110 First Lady McKinley
111 "That guy's got some tree goo!"?
115 Moon of Jupiter
117 Storage containers
119 Droop from underwatering
120 Leading man and lady's noggins?
122 Ma with Grammys
123 Pennsylvania port
124 Puppet pal of Kukla
125 Bout of excess
126 Visa competitor, for short
127 Symbol on some Sneetches
128 They're board
129 National-anthem start

Down

1 Seated yoga position
2 Yemeni's eastern neighbor
3 Sent copy by phone
4 "Take __ Train"
5 In the past
6 Mea __
7 Lie low
8 Place of bliss
9 1994 Depp film "Don Juan __" ("Comrade" anagram)
10 Violin virtuoso Shlomo
11 Love to pieces
12 Gray-day array
13 Match up, in a way
14 Rap-sheet abbr.
15 One might be used to restore a fireplace structure?
16 Being pulled along
17 Kroft of "60 Minutes"
19 Evaluated
24 Regency brand hotels, e.g.
29 Bert of Cowardly Lion fame
30 Bauhaus artist Paul
34 "Cats" cat Rum __ Tugger
37 Cutlass carmaker
38 "Geraldo at Large" host
39 According to
40 Co. touted by Nipper
42 Teammate of Vixen, Comet, etc.
43 French vineyards
44 Source of rope or dope
45 West country?
46 Out on the deep
47 "Sans" opposite
48 Spirited ditty
50 Parisian hub
51 Word with red or ticker
55 Rip into
58 Egyptian sacred beetle
59 Bring on staff
60 Simile phrase
63 "Liberty Enlightening the World", et al.
64 Jazz contralto James
65 Diet-cola brand since 1963
68 "Nova" subj.
71 Yalta's peninsula
72 Extremity
73 Worshipped one
75 Commoner
76 Ireland, on its euro coins
77 Graph-paper configurations
78 Asian cold desert
80 French 101 infinitive
81 Cries of surprise
85 Laundry basins
87 Joint "taken" by some NFL players
89 Bog
90 More wily
92 Sprint
94 Hammer-wielding god
95 AT&T's industry
96 Vehicle for moves
98 Many a marathon memento
101 Benghazi's land
102 "Buy the farm", e.g.
104 Shire of "Rocky"
105 Blender brand
106 Prior to
107 Skyrockets
108 Sleep-time breathing disorder
109 Stengel or Kasem
112 Ladies who lamb
113 Pump part
114 Cuba, por ejemplo
116 Bank takeback, briefly
118 They're Red or White on diamonds
121 Loser to D.D.E.

44

Griddy Sounds

Across

1 Item in a quiver
6 Figurative brink
9 Play for time
14 Emmy category
19 Nikon alternative
20 Pen point
21 Certain Ivy Leaguer
22 One enjoying a joint, maybe
23 Horse blankets for those not in the race?
26 Bout of excess
27 One of six for Henry VIII
28 Fireplace tool
29 Bleachers' features
31 Prez after Harry
32 Part of a skateboarding feat?
37 Joe serving
40 Equivalent of -speak
41 Natural hair-bleacher
42 In a creepy way
43 Fragile atmospheric layer
45 Salts away
48 Sugar source
49 The sea, in "The Old Man and the Sea"?
53 Freedom from burdens
57 "Tiger in your tank" brand
58 Baseball's Hammerin' Hank
59 Ailment that causes trembling?
63 Imposing dwellings
66 Jouster's mount
67 In the style of
68 Atlantic City venues
71 Vacuum's lack
73 Spielberg film/ship name
75 Spanish eye
76 Diplomat Root
79 Arrange in columns and rows
82 Result of dropping one's cell phone in a puddle?
85 Whiz
86 The whole shebang
90 Cookie "born" in New York's Chelsea
91 Sheep's cry to its sheepdog?
94 Magna ——
98 Intelligent society
99 Like some elephants
100 British-style clothier
102 Homer Simpson's pop
103 Fall behind
105 Big 'do
106 Conversations surrounding kids' modeling clay?
112 Giants right fielder Mel
113 Sleep: prefix
114 Vital vascular vessel
115 Cathedral recess
119 Forerunner of bridge
121 Sweet 'n salty snack?
125 Kia's Korean home
126 Upright
127 Uncle, in Uruguay
128 "Family Guy" dad
129 Orange-colored Muppet
130 Physicist for whom a coil is named
131 VIP on the Hill
132 Brand now under Whirlpool

Down

1 Keep —— profile
2 Mortgage payoff switch, briefly
3 Jazz motif
4 TV's Brady Bunch was one
5 Realm of Ares
6 Concert bonus
7 "It Must Be Him" singer Carr
8 Flowed back
9 Early Pink Floyd member Barrett
10 Smidgen
11 Pulitzer-winning novelist Lurie
12 Fabric from flax
13 Will beneficiary
14 Dinner wrap?
15 Emulate Nelly
16 Of a heart chamber
17 In a humble manner
18 Spinning dizzily
24 Bonobos and gibbons
25 Verdi aria "—— tu"
30 Quaker pronoun
33 Bread end
34 Minute fraction: abbr.
35 Wind blasts
36 Older partner?
37 —— d'Azur
38 Yom Kippur War weapons
39 Okra's are sticky
44 A Judd
45 Kolkata wrap
46 Buck's tail?
47 Game show letter-turner
48 Champagne specification
50 Kind of cooking oil
51 Jewish sect member: var.
52 Responses akin to "Say what?"
54 Blind as ——
55 Toni Morrison novel
56 Quaint "OMG!"
60 Narc's target
61 Insist on
62 Perfect for publication
64 Over again
65 It may precede "Stay!"
68 Gabrielle Chanel, by nickname
69 Cracked open
70 Shoe part
72 Japanese noodle dish
74 Penn and Connery
77 "Howdy!"
78 Mattel card game
80 Scrooge sounds
81 Eye layer
83 Like some subway trains
84 Louisiana-style stew
87 End-of-week "Yay!"
88 Actor Epps
89 Greek founder of Stoicism
92 Coral composition
93 "Othello" villain
95 Last Supper guest
96 —— Park, Queens
97 Louis Armstrong's instrument
100 Tizzy
101 Mete out
102 Parenthetical comments
103 English author Edward Bulwer——
104 A wife of Esau
106 Use a divining rod
107 Toughen
108 Thumbs-down review
109 Plunders
110 Golfer Palmer, familiarly
111 Sultan's women
116 Gyro bread
117 British WWII gun
118 Pound who penned "The Cantos"
120 Fashion designer Anna
122 LXV x X
123 Suffix with señor
124 MPG rating group

Comic Con

Across
1 Root-beer brand
6 Summits
11 Symbols of Egyptian royalty
15 Maharani's wrap
19 Slobs' digs
20 Avian perch
21 Bygone Persian title
22 Footnote ditto, briefly
23 Culinary fare that leaves one baffled?
26 Old King Cole request
27 Draft status
28 Part of kWh
29 Diverse: prefix
30 Pasture
31 Skin pic
33 Place where the nuns are windbags?
39 Wily
40 Bric-a-___
43 Ashen
44 Mortgage holder, e.g.
45 Parents who give mixed messages?
50 Fireplace, to Burns
53 Recipe amts.
54 Sweetheart of 98-Down
55 The Big Easy: abbr.
56 Frost or Pound
57 Cot alternative
59 Collar maker?
62 What one might eat on a really long airport layover?
67 "Yo, Nero!"
68 Nueva York, por ejemplo
69 "Kapow!"
70 Basic juicing tool
72 Grammy winner ___ Lo Green
73 Potential winners who are actually wimps?
80 NFL stats
81 Stadium levels
82 Actress Charlotte et al.
83 Numskull
84 Singer Cleo or Frankie
86 "___ Misbehavin'"
87 Quark-antiquark particle
88 What snobs might be listed in, on a roster?
95 Chooses
96 Prefix meaning green
97 Comes out with
98 Maven
101 Sign above the counter of a green grocer?
106 Body of water surrounding Venice, e.g.
108 Make an effort
109 Margarine, quaintly
110 Fashion finish?
113 Numbered musical work
114 Some European deer
116 Very hard place to visit in the Mediterranean?
120 "Out of Africa" author Dinesen
121 Forked over
122 Ready in the keg
123 To date
124 Mrs. Dithers in "Blondie"
125 Keats creations
126 "Seinfeld" character ___ Kramer
127 Plants used for thatching

Down
1 Kin of cravats
2 Unkeyed, musically
3 Minutes in a soccer game
4 Trim, as meat
5 Sch. with a Spokane campus
6 Oratorio solo
7 Geezer
8 Shevat or Sha'ban, e.g.
9 PC bailout key
10 Apt name for a cook?
11 Very, to Verdi
12 Bake, as eggs
13 Freak out from fear
14 Yonder yacht
15 Sambuca sample
16 Eisenhower library's Kansas city
17 Aging agent
18 Forms thoughts
24 Like court testimony
25 Russian prince a.k.a. "Moneybag"
32 Winds member
34 Fesses (up)
35 Smidgen
36 Sainted Norwegian king
37 TV's Nick at ___
38 ATV or SUV
41 "Flow gently, sweet ___": Burns
42 Trig ratio
45 Barton in nursing history
46 Not exceeding
47 Ti or mi
48 Latch (onto)
49 Pen point type
50 Contaminate
51 Readied for the gallows
52 Bum muscles
56 "Hunny"-loving bear
57 Dutch painter Hals
58 Gomer Pyle's grp.
59 Small parts for big stars
60 Carry to excess
61 Human being
63 Agcy. concerned with epidemics
64 Cab alternative, nowadays
65 Deity akin to Mars
66 Spy novelist Deighton
71 Calculating viper?
74 Arthr- suffix meaning inflamed
75 Cannes showing
76 Acute
77 Not an imit.
78 iPods after Minis
79 Colorful aquarium fish
84 Jared of "Dallas Buyers Club"
85 Org.
86 Erelong
87 Small plateau
88 Suffix with ego
89 Fragrant, dark sherry
90 It starts with a dropped ball?
91 LXX x X
92 Type of cattle and scones
93 Here, to Henri
94 "Lay Lady Lay" singer
98 Foe of Bluto
99 Sent via a specified path
100 Initial occurrences
102 "Such a pity!"
103 "Dallas" matriarch
104 Takes "People" in
105 Boxfuls at showers
107 Yellow-flowered prickly shrub
111 Con job
112 "___ the mornin'!"
115 Jamaican music genre
116 NYSE debut
117 Specs-wearing Disney dwarf
118 Beatle bride of 1969
119 Tesla product

Thanksgiving Leftovers

Each of the answers to the starred clues is still correct with one letter removed. Find the 18 "leftovers" (that is, the dropped letters) and rearrange them to form a three-word message.

Across

1 Pup
6 Caribbean resort island
11 *Shore bird
15 "House" actor Omar
19 Certain IM user
20 Cyrus of twerking notoriety
21 Dog-food brand
22 Fat-based bird treat
23 *Black bird representation, perhaps
25 *One in a green fruit-bearing grove
27 Beethoven's "Kreutzer", e.g.
28 Not final, in law
30 Sample
31 Puzzle with an eye for an I, say
34 *Refreshing brew
39 Abbr. on Bermuda skeds
42 "What's —— like?"
44 Deems to be
45 *Feature of some rainstorms
48 Poets
49 Actress Sorvino
53 Coyote cries
54 Kind of admiral
55 Botanical burn-soother
56 Salts away
57 Modern pentathlon weapon
58 Having a twisty path
60 *Nickname for a group of actors
62 *Female first name
64 Mare hair
65 Gofer's tasks
66 Docs who deliver
68 Belgian city ("unarm" anagram)
71 Agnus —— (Lamb of God)
72 Yet to come
76 Mountain ht.
78 *Zero
83 *Paid trainees, e.g.
85 Distribute, as a pamphlet
87 Radiance
88 Collegian a.k.a. Eli
89 Periodic-table fig.
91 "Take —— from me"
92 Genetic copy
93 Roman : Mars :: Greek : ——
94 Like some swarms
95 *Formula One competitor
97 Eternal
99 Blues or bluegrass
100 Psychic's subj.
101 *Apt name for a photo biz
106 Winter falls
108 Golfer Palmer, familiarly
109 Some, in Spain
111 Limited to a single instance
115 *Wash-day challenge
120 *Do a correspondence task
123 Part of IHOP: abbr.
124 Wield power
125 Silent performers
126 Jazz pianist Chick
127 Katharine of "The Graduate"
128 *Xerox has two
129 Etching fluids
130 Sheepshanks, e.g.

Down

1 Tail motions
2 Time-related prefix with scope
3 Personal flair
4 "Roots" actor Burton
5 Makes believe
6 French friend
7 Canyon edge
8 —— Bator, Mongolia
9 Kick off
10 "Yes, captain!"
11 "Way", in Confucianism
12 Building annex
13 Troy, N.Y., sch.
14 Veterans Day mo.
15 Cornerstone abbr.
16 Prize money
17 Pro golfer Calvin ——
18 Take the helm
24 Bigwig
26 Approx. takeoff hrs.
29 Cold pack
32 *No-no on some road signs
33 Unbroken flow
35 Same: Fr.
36 Chocolate alternative
37 Commanded
38 Mormons, for short
39 Feels sore
40 Gradient
41 After-bath need
43 Native of an 85-Down metropolis
46 "Gold" Peter Fonda title role
47 Fashion designer —— Turk
49 Route chart: Sp.
50 *Male first name
51 In-basket stamp: abbr.
52 Says "Who?"
56 Narrow groove
58 Buffalo hockey player
59 Where Hercules slew the lion
61 "Well, —— you special?"
63 Nary a soul
67 Mexican shawls
69 Of a forearm bone
70 Discount label, often
72 Hockey player Kovalchuk
73 Close by
74 *Something rung up at a pub
75 Cooperstown's —— Speaker
77 Expresses
79 Aptly named citrus fruit
80 Mitt
81 Fine-tunes
82 Annoying little punk
84 Long-legged wader
85 Japan's main island
86 *Abbr. for a Keystone State sch.
90 Glasgow vetoes
92 Collarless pullover type
94 Suffix with broker or shrink
96 Show hunger
97 $5 bills, slangily
98 California wine valley
101 Arafat in Palestinian history
102 University of Maine's home
103 Lesson segments
104 Small brooks
105 Discussion subject
107 —— fire (ignite)
110 Road rig
112 Other, in Oaxaca
113 They fill some pumps
114 Italian monks' titles
116 III, in Roma
117 "La Cage —— Folles"
118 Land in la mer
119 Old game-console inits.
121 Hollywood's Beatty
122 Biblical beast

Season to Be Punny

Across

1 Networks
5 Made public
10 Religious ascetic
14 Historic Harlem ballroom
19 Neck of the woods
20 Geography-class object
21 Mayberry boy
22 Justice Kagan
23 With 33-Across, line one of an original verse
26 Pulitzer-winning composer Ned
27 Not digital
28 Wettish
29 Earlier
31 Linguist Chomsky
33 See 23-Across
38 A lot of sass?
42 Stallone's "First Blood" role
45 Gen- —— (post-boomer set)
46 Bronx attraction
47 India's first prime minister
48 "Believe —— not!"
49 "The Cable Guy" Carrey
50 Waldorf and Caesar
53 Line two of the verse
57 Actress Zellweger
58 Invited
59 Frat-party buy
60 Meltable shelters
62 Stow, as cargo
63 Like the lumbar spine's lower neighbor
67 Taken in a heist
69 Tarzan portrayer Ron
70 With 84-Across, line three of the verse
72 Highlands hat
75 Parsons' dwellings
76 Sun circler
77 Prefix meaning half
78 In short supply
80 General on Chinese menus
81 Hags
83 Anvil-striking sound
84 See 70-Across
90 Yellow jacket's relative
92 Profs' helpers
93 Have the nerve
94 Wish-granter in "Aladdin"
95 Nile biter
96 AAA suggestions
98 To be, to Spaniards
99 Couldn't stand
100 With 117-Across, line four of the verse
104 Fly catcher?
106 Illustrious
107 Singer Ronstadt
110 Treat table salt
115 "Gloria ——" (hymn)
117 See 100-Across
121 Tightfisted
122 Yen
123 State known for lobster
124 Facts and figures
125 Poets à la Shakespeare
126 Cribbage markers
127 Spanish folk hero
128 Poetry competition

Down

1 Gilda Radner role Baba ——
2 Moran of "Happy Days"
3 Second Greek letter
4 Comedian Mort
5 Early disco, the Whisky ——
6 Off one's feed
7 Dorm co-habitant, e.g.
8 River through Zaragoza
9 Lucy's costar
10 Ramadan or Elul
11 Make a decision
12 Fed. bio-med. research agcy.
13 Caretaker
14 Sans- —— (typeface)
15 Emotionally remote
16 New York Harbor's —— -Narrows Bridge
17 Undivided
18 Starchy Thanksgiving item
24 Ingest
25 Meaning of a colon, in analogies
30 Politician Perot
32 Bone-dry
34 Way off the highway
35 Internet —— (viral phenomenon)
36 Mine bonanzas
37 Win at dieting
38 Empower
39 Soap opera, say
40 Poorly constructed
41 Wear away
43 Slip-on shoe, for short
44 NBC news veteran Tom
49 Spree
51 Thirty-year senator Specter
52 Spinks in boxing history
54 Working together precisely
55 Recovery setback
56 The D in LED
61 Technological snag
64 Braying equines
65 British runner Sebastian ——
66 Hosp. professionals
67 Reggae precursor
68 Lacrosse team complement
70 Bart, Lisa, and Maggie's mom
71 London insurer of Grable's legs
72 Apartment renter
73 2001 French film starring Audrey Tautou
74 Deluded
75 "Buddenbrooks" author
77 Book after Daniel
78 Wade noisily
79 Cabinetmaker, e.g.
80 Some are high-def
82 "For sure, man!"
83 Shoot the breeze
85 The Sun Bowl's sch.
86 Coarse file
87 "Dig in!"
88 Theatrical
89 Hatcher of "Desperate Housewives"
91 Like this puzzle's verse
97 Do some de-cluttering
98 Emmy-winning Falco
101 Santa-tracking org.
102 Swabs made by Unilever
103 North Pole workers
105 Measured via stopwatch
108 Birth certificate entry
109 Twofold
111 June honorees
112 Romance lang.
113 Catherine —— - Jones
114 Red-clad Dutch cheese
115 Banned toxic compound: abbr.
116 "I knew it!"
118 Mesabi Range deposit
119 Sheepskin boots brand
120 Prefix with sex or corn

48

You Get an A!

Across

1 Priest's robe
4 Total flop
8 Anatomical pouches
12 Pal of Pooh
18 Black goo
19 Washstand vessel
20 Balm ingredient
21 Rather poky
22 Country that has nothing?
25 Former Defense Secretary Leon
26 Corn Belt state
27 "Ol' Blue Eyes"
28 Genetic anomaly
29 Island of El Greco's birth
31 Clearasil target
32 Sherry alternative
33 HDTV screen type
36 Feast during Nisan
37 Be a victim of paint theft?
42 Tease
44 Cream of the crop
45 "Rodeo" composer Copland
46 Life story in a nutshell
49 Eye doctor's witticism?
54 Up next
55 Number after sieben
57 Praiseful hymn
58 Hose
60 Actress Ruby
61 Vegan staple
62 Grounds
64 Freeloader
66 Uppity sort
67 Designerwear for Bossy's set?
71 Pewter element
74 Transplant, as houseplants
76 Fragment
77 Golden Rule preposition
78 5 ml. amt.
80 Do some fightin'
84 Taco-salad "dressing"
86 Slaughter who played for the Yankees
87 Twenty Questions category
89 What sticky eyelashes might feel like?
92 Bonobo, e.g.
93 On a scale of one ——
94 Elevator-company name
95 Carol Burnett tugged hers as a sign-off
97 Moth's path to a meal, maybe?
104 Mooring site
108 M.O.
109 A in music?
110 Turn off course
111 Paramour
112 Edges laterally
115 Feature of some summer shoes
118 Lady of La Mancha
119 Car-deal component
121 Song line of 27-Across adapted by a Yucatán native?
123 Home of the A's
124 Nevada betting setting
125 Croft played by Angelina
126 Summer, to Yves
127 "——Playing Our Song"
128 Yemen's Gulf of ——
129 Glimpse
130 Billy Ray, to Miley

Down

1 Storage stories, often
2 Punjab's capital
3 Made coffee or beer
4 "Maude" star Arthur
5 Has
6 Toward a central axis
7 Rodeo ride
8 South Carolina river
9 Banned fruit spray
10 Musical closing passage
11 SpongeBob's habitat
12 Major Missouri tributary
13 New Rochelle college
14 Singer Stefani
15 Not much of a hair-dye color?
16 Ballpark fig.
17 Article in rap titles
21 Gush
23 "See ya!"
24 Lady Gaga calls hers "little monsters"
28 Zero with three Tonys
30 Holder in Obama's cabinet
32 Annoying
34 "Time in a Bottle" singer Jim
35 German thanks
38 Transitive vb. follower
39 Former Dodge
40 Parson's residence
41 Place to crash
43 Jazz style
46 Loony
47 Clickable image
48 Response to "Why are you making that flatbread?"?
50 Clerical shirtfronts
51 "Swell!"
52 90 degrees
53 Indigo dye source
54 Definitely draftable
56 Telly, on our side of the pond
59 Firstborn
63 Third-quarter mo.
65 Whodunit game
67 Frosty's eyes
68 Tilting-tower town
69 Harvest
70 Rights org.
72 Resting on
73 Prescription amount
75 Short-sheeting, e.g.
78 Affected goodbyes
79 Like some wet blankets?
81 Sir Walter and Sir Ridley
82 Willowy
83 "Night" author Wiesel
85 Put away, in a way
88 Funnyman Brooks
90 Means of WWW access
91 Southern-sounding sailboat
96 Valerie Harper sitcom
98 Waiting at the bank, say
99 Exceedingly
100 Photographer Richard
101 Prefix meaning kidney
102 What the pot may call black?
103 Pizzeria lures
105 Proclaimed
106 Longtime Met soprano Scotto
107 Worn at the edges
113 In a slothful way
114 Beloved
115 Had too much, briefly
116 Tree in Maine's nickname
117 Tombstone lawman
119 Rugrat
120 Cheerleader's cry
121 Gershwin or Glass
122 Cheerleader's cry

49

Split Seconds

Across

1 Hiking route
6 Mister, en Espanol
11 Wolf group
15 Go (through) ploddingly
19 Sun-dried brick
20 Erenow
21 "Camelot" lyricist Lerner
22 Modest skirt
23 Scrapes the windshield in winter?
25 Jimmy Durante prominence
26 Strings strummed in HI
27 Flood barrier
28 Polite man is dissuaded by everyone?
31 Dept. of Justice agency
33 This: Sp.
35 Entered by careful maneuvering
36 Bug-drone runs off with a queen?
40 Poultry drumsticks
43 Blue —— (plants used for tequila)
44 Book before Luke
45 Eradicates
49 Less naughty
50 Look after
52 River through Bern
53 Fair to middling
54 What squids squirt
55 Choice of fruit vs. vegetable?
58 Accomplished
59 Some cropped pants
62 Trim that may be faux
63 Biased
65 Ancient Nile Valley region
66 Looney Tunes "devil", briefly
69 Prefix with natal
71 Stories of the gods
72 Downright stupid
74 Chem experiment site
76 Sampras rival Andre
78 Bruins Hall of Famer Bobby
79 Those in a wonderful shoe family?
83 Org. Heston once headed
86 Mouth, slangily
88 Smidgen
89 Madame Gorbachev
90 Invite to one's penthouse, say
92 Diagnostic tool for tuberculosis
94 Key in a sea
95 Fictional Plaza Hotel imp
96 Pentagram
97 Relatively short, as songs go?
100 Rummy variety
104 Cruise-Holmes daughter
105 Some NFL linemen
106 Phony one's got to be hurting?
111 Prince of Darkness
113 —— even keel

114 Alternative to Ivory
115 Sculptures, e.g., that the Simpsons' disco guy damages?
120 Start to freeze?
121 "Passages" author Sheehy
122 New staffer
123 Appropriate forcibly
124 Unassuming
125 Termini
126 They have low pH's
127 Writing assignment, often

Down

1 Bit of bod ink
2 Nutritional amt.
3 NASA "thumbs-up"
4 What "credo" means
5 —— -majesté (treason)
6 Most secure
7 Lacking vigor
8 "There is —— in team"
9 Shamu, for one
10 Bobbin
11 Black-and-white bamboo eaters
12 Healing succulent plants
13 Societal division
14 Hit with a leg joint
15 Undue self-satisfaction
16 Michigan, e.g
17 Plow team
18 Crux

24 Tandoors and kilns
29 Onion relative
30 Get one's dander (up)
31 "Oliver Twist" villain
32 Tirade of a Rottweiler-colored mongrel?
34 Pre-Maya Mexican
36 Salon service similar to a pedi
37 —— Lingus
38 Inauguration vow
39 Validation
41 Wenceslas after a diet?
42 "Rugrats" girl and others
45 Cartoonish baby cry
46 Income sources for golden yrs.
47 Rhea of "Cheers"
48 Sondheim's Sweeney
50 Cinque + uno
51 River the Brooklyn Bridge crosses
52 Real-estate unit
55 Setting for Laura Ingalls Wilder
56 Tenure on Broadway, say
57 Popular work shift
60 Blood-typing letters
61 Worrisome engine sound
64 Windows systems that debuted in 1993: abbr.
65 Hockey trophy with 78-Across's name in it, aptly
67 Baja's opposite
68 Nuke in the microwave
70 Wine-cask woods
72 Manhattan Chinatown street
73 Corp. bigwigs
75 Joint-cushioning sac
77 Actress Scala
80 Courtroom VIP
81 Shopping-spree site
82 Beer first brewed in Brooklyn
84 Ploys
85 Big brutes
87 Antiwar demonstrator
90 PC key near Ctrl
91 Vinegar trait
93 Miner's railcar
94 Desktop Apple
95 Verdi aria, literally: "It was you"
97 Purposely delays
98 Sounded fretful
99 Gives an address
101 Gentle push
102 Like some elephants
103 Prim and proper
106 Lather
107 Hollywood's Hathaway
108 Sister of Pippa
109 "I get the pun!"
110 "Spamalot" creator Idle
112 Together, in scores
116 Half of hex-
117 Greek consonants
118 Song syllable
119 One might bug you?

Bad Hair-Pun Day

Across

1 Long-tailed, colorful parrot
6 iPhone's virtual assistant
10 Possesses
13 Cosmetician Elizabeth
18 Thompson, a.k.a. Honey Boo Boo
19 Tool for crimping or straightening
20 —— Raton, Florida
21 Nobelist Curie
22 They go easy on your hair at the salon?
25 Brand under Whirlpool
26 Sacred scrolls
27 Jimi Hendrix's hair, right after a shampoo?
29 Holy hombre, in place names
30 Ring ref's calls
33 Grain bristle
34 Desktop image
35 Amounts, in physics
37 Designer von Fürstenberg
40 Makes by hand
44 Role for a mortuary hairstylist?
48 Needing darning
50 Home builder's buy
51 Flak from a flock?
52 Jeté, say
53 Taj Mahal's city
54 Top-shelf
55 Yellowfin tuna
56 Latin 101 verb
58 1980 Diana Ross hit adapted for hairstylists?
62 Seeks, as office
64 Sammy Davis Jr. book "—— Can"
65 Tara and Tim in acting
66 Apt response to one who's cut your hair?
71 Nixon Defense secretary Melvin
72 Symbol of saintliness
73 Panhandlers
76 Prescription for healthier hair?
79 Vincent van ——
80 20 percent, maybe
81 What Easter ends
82 Savvy about
83 American-born Jordanian queen
85 Tennis's Sampras
86 Bowl over
87 Basil-based Italian sauce
89 Kind of list for a great hairstylist's clients?
92 Civil-rights activist Evers
94 Predatory sea mammal
96 Like finger paints
97 Part of U.A.E.
99 "I knew it!"
101 Icelandic literary work
102 Frequently, poetically
105 Extensions that make hair feel like straw?
111 Make certain
113 Consumed
114 Reason to get another perm?
117 Brook catch
118 Like the French Open's courts
119 Where icicles may form
120 Went ballistic
121 Hair-salon sounds
122 Tarzan portrayer Ron
123 He lost with Romney in 2012
124 Atlanta university

Down

1 Sail supports
2 Metal biz with the NYSE symbol AA
3 Terrier type
4 Anatomical loop (Lat. "handle")
5 Clothes might be soaked in one
6 Round Table title
7 Its workers have taxing jobs: abbr.?
8 Santa's landing surface
9 Prefix meaning "below"
10 Vuvuzela, e.g.
11 No. on a statement
12 Utter a casual greeting
13 Passionate
14 Beverly Cleary heroine —— Quimby
15 Lure
16 German article
17 Longtime NPR host Conan
20 Creature
23 Herr Schindler
24 Groundskeeper's machine
28 Latin "Look!"
31 Just for fun
32 Pigpens
35 NFL's Mannings, e.g.: abbr.
36 Org. of cavity-fillers
38 "My goodness!"
39 Well-adjusted person, slangily
41 River-flow controls
42 Muscle tension, in medicine
43 Editor's "Let it be"
44 Ski-lift type
45 Pearl Harbor's island
46 Kept up
47 Prefix with dermis
49 Chem experiment site
53 Breezes through
54 Lifelong process
56 "Old MacDonald had ——..."
57 "Le ——" (Paris newspaper)
59 "Myra Breckinridge" sequel
60 Abbr. re flawed mdse.
61 Horse's "Hey!"
63 Caps Lock neighbor
67 Japanese "way of the gods"
68 Contributing element
69 Miscellany
70 Scrubbed, as a launch
71 Lerner's musical partner
74 Baby dedication, e.g.
75 Made tracks
76 Kind of chowder
77 Clipped hairstyles?
78 67.5 deg., on a compass
79 "I'm stumped"
84 CIA forerunner
85 "Gangnam Style" singer
87 They get you going?
88 Prominent periods
89 Religion founded in Persia
90 Weather-surveillance tool
91 Doodle deletion, say
93 Relinquished
95 "You're So Vain" singer Simon
98 Italian lawn game
100 "Lou Grant" star
102 Expenditure
103 Less inhibited
104 One-piece lingerie item
105 Dampens
106 Merit
107 Yours, to Yves
108 At capacity
109 "Salt and pepper" ingredient?
110 Stick around
112 In-box or lunch-box stuff
115 A Gabor sister
116 Stimpy's cartoon pal

Project Roadway

Across

1 Crude calculators
6 Denials in Dundee
10 Like grass at dawn
14 Sapient
18 A Williams at Wimbledon
20 Of little —— use
21 Cinco + tres
22 Bad day for Caesar
23 Some dresses fitting a super-thin model?
25 Boxer Ali, formerly
26 Salon application
27 Evaluates
28 Distant kin of leg-warmers?
31 Salon application
32 Book after Gen.
34 Character actor Wallach
35 Anouk or Mann
36 Advice for bedecking the neck?
42 "R.U.R." playwright Capek
45 Gateway Arch architect Saarinen
46 Frank McCourt memoir
47 Gives birth to
50 Uniform's shoulder adornment
53 Put finishing touches on a cami alternative?
58 CCLI, doubled
59 Imelda into shoes
61 Folkie Woody's son
62 River dividing Paris
63 San Francisco Peninsula city
65 Half of a tot's train-sound
66 Goad
67 Slip into
68 Shoes that are a source of power?
72 A thousand thou
73 Spanish Surrealist Joan
75 Exemplar of thinness
76 Blissful place
80 Fragile atmospheric layer
82 Eliminate from "The Apprentice"
83 Fashioned
85 Actress Vardalos or Peebles
86 Snaps open a handheld purse?
89 Gridiron complements
91 They work on the "Elle" words: abbr.
92 Jiffy Lube supply
93 Charismatic radiance
95 In a stew
96 Wholesaler's headwear?
102 Staggering
105 67.5 deg., on a compass
106 "Dracula" creator Stoker
107 Forlorn
110 Knitting details on a type of sleeveless dress?
115 Put on a pedestal
118 Theater award established by "The Village Voice"
119 Mythical ship of Jason
120 Sports jacket for a Chase?
122 Ceramist's oven
123 Parch
124 Bar mitzvah dance
125 Slowly or surely, e.g.
126 Scraped (out), as a living
127 Station below MSG
128 Iridescent gemstone
129 Test, as ore

Down

1 Syrian president
2 First name in flagmaking
3 Crop up
4 Gospel singer Winans
5 Rubber-stamping supplies
6 Sickening
7 Pound sound
8 ——'acte
9 Former Cubs star Sammy
10 Mild-mannered
11 Patisserie treat
12 "Come again?"
13 Ma with many a Grammy
14 Definitely hip
15 "Dressed to the nines" is one
16 Have a hunch
17 Cosmetician Lauder
19 Great trait
24 Twice tri-
29 Second-smallest state: abbr.
30 Hikes workers like
33 On account of
36 Little: Fr.
37 Tracey of "Small Time Crooks"
38 High-profile dos, for short
39 Natty dresser
40 Bus driver on "The Simpsons"
41 Med. research funder
42 Sneakers brand
43 Samoa's capital
44 Beads on open umbrellas
47 Some have widows' peaks
48 Part of A.D.
49 Timetable, briefly
51 Scarf down
52 Nonkosher
54 Honolulu's island
55 Gift tag word
56 Hanging flexibly, as hats
57 Lukewarm
60 Katie with ABC News
64 Natural satellites
65 Lowest-ranking NCO
69 British peer
70 In —— of (replacing)
71 Black Friday event
72 Fabricated
73 Look glum
74 Polo Ralph Lauren rival
77 Seminary subj.
78 Trigonometry function
79 It's right on most maps
81 Star, in Paris
82 Fedora material
83 —— work (drudgery)
84 Rhythmic pulsation
87 Informal greetings
88 Letter after sigma
90 No. 2 execs
94 Coming
96 Rely
97 Carter's White House successor
98 Hardwired, as a genetic trait
99 Its cap. is Brussels
100 Suffragist Elizabeth —— Stanton
101 Unicellular "shape-shifter"
102 "Is this some kind of ——?"
103 Man with a trademarked cube
104 Author Zola
107 Numbers on some trunks
108 Hyundai sedan model
109 Hat a.k.a. bowler
111 Grating sound
112 Native Canadian
113 Sonar comeback
114 Boutique
116 Radar : Burghoff :: Hawkeye : ——
117 Restrooms, informally
121 We're in the Cenozoic one

It's How You Say It

Across

1 MetLife Stadium team
5 Sometimes-deviated nasal parts
10 Former senator Lott
15 False god
19 False god
20 Org. that tracks Santa
21 Psalms interjection
22 Do that's picked
23 Thumbelina, e.g.?
25 Away at a mini-golf course?
27 Thwart
28 Robert who played A.J. Soprano
30 —— dixit
31 Orinoco or Ebro, por ejemplo
32 Word after Mardi or foie
34 Nary a soul
37 Bolts
39 Give a play's star the ax?
44 Spot for a nosh
46 Hyundai model
47 French : eau :: German : ——
49 Bounding strides
52 Fodder keeper
53 Do a checkout task
55 Proverbial company, fighting?
58 Sea seasoning
59 Heal, as fractures
61 Part of M.I.T.
62 Ready to eat
63 Beginnings
66 Downright dopey
69 Most breezy
71 A fish who pulls some strings?
75 Publish anew
79 Digging tool
80 Parkway strip
85 Composer Khachaturian
86 "Closing Bell" network
89 Type of division
91 Ancient Andean
92 Slogan for durable clothing?
96 Traffic jam sound
98 Grad
99 Schindler with a list
100 Bewitched state
102 Just-born baby
104 "Tiger in your tank" brand
106 Furniture artist?
108 Bog
111 Open, as envelopes
113 Bridal accessory
114 Old name for Tokyo
115 "I could —— horse!"
117 Lotto-like game
119 Strong-arm
124 A tailor might play them?
128 Kites, e.g.?
130 Louver part
131 Goes after
132 —— sanctum
133 Parks who wouldn't stand for segregation
134 Cravings
135 Ruhr valley city
136 Teacher's "We need to talk"
137 Ides rebuke

Down

1 Music's Croce and Morrison
2 Polish text
3 "Monk" star Shalhoub
4 Squalid urban area
5 Those showing scorn
6 Dec. or Jan. 31, e.g.
7 Pat on the back
8 Manx cat's lack
9 Back matter
10 Chinese menu general
11 KO caller
12 Pixie-like
13 Emulated a cat, in a way
14 Consequently
15 It's swung over a plate
16 In flames
17 Golfer Palmer, familiarly
18 Nike's swoosh and such
24 Stingy
26 Nonstick surface
29 Avian perch
33 "Oh, woe!"
35 Keister
36 Cheri formerly on "SNL"
38 Island group off Sicily
39 Bas-relief mixture
40 Cuban boy in 2000 news
41 Some Starbucks sizes
42 U.S. govt. security
43 Window-shopper shader
45 Snobbery
48 Nickelodeon cartoon pooch
50 Canal of song
51 Soaks (up)
54 Spanish liqueur
56 Actor Morales
57 Moisten
60 Greek consonants
64 TV sta. with a "very funny" slogan
65 Cup holders
67 Playful bite
68 Bibliography abbr.
70 Hwy.
72 FedExed, say
73 Pueblo building-blocks
74 Russo of "Ransom"
75 Tried for office
76 Suffix with smack or switch
77 Pet food brand
78 Enjoys a Havana
81 Supreme who played Dorothy in "The Wiz"
82 Pippa Middleton, to Prince William
83 Less than 90 degrees
84 Christener, e.g.
87 Put bread on a thoroughbred?
88 2011 World Series champs, briefly
90 Literary category
93 Bacon portion
94 Scarce
95 Move stealthily
97 A treat for feet
101 Creator of Narnia
103 Low deck on a ship
105 Some belly buttons
107 Tennis's Goolagong
108 Unkempt
109 "Rolling in the Deep" singer
110 "Laugh-In" co-host
112 Scruffs
116 Cathedral recess
118 Digits in a 127-Down
120 To be, to Flaubert
121 Radish or turnip, e.g.
122 Sac that may be pathological
123 Twin in Genesis
125 UFO crew
126 —— out a living
127 I.D. with two hyphens
129 Like Gov. Cuomo: abbr.

The puzzle on the following page was created by Stephen Sondheim for *New York*'s debut issue in 1968. It's of the type known as a cryptic, or British-style crossword, in which each clue conveys the answer twice: once straightforwardly, by a more or less conventional definition, and secondarily through a piece of wordplay or humor. The latter treatment is meant to obscure and reveal simultaneously.

Cryptic crosswords can seem baffling to neophytes, so Sondheim, in that first issue of *New York*, included a primer. His enthusiastic, detailed guide—really the best you'll find—is titled "How to Do a *Real* Crossword Puzzle (Or What's a Four-Letter Word for 'East Indian Betel Nut' and Who Cares?)." It's available at nymag.com/sondheimpuzzle.

New York Magazine Puzzle

By Stephen Sondheim

Clues

ACROSS

1 *Theme-word A* (8). *Variations:* 13 (4) and 36 (4)
11 Entertain and wind again? (6)
14 "Foremen Do" —poem in Old English (7)
18 Is it unnecessary to want fewer things? (8)
19 The straight prefix bit—ha! (5)
21 What's gone by sounds like it went by (4)
22 "Tramp, tramp, tramp"—a catchphrase (6)
24 *Theme-word B* (6). *Variations:* 28 (5) and 8 Ac. (4)

26 Heavy wig they messed up (7)
27 Uproot the house plant at the station? (5)
29 This Unit is still part of the Resistance (3)
31 *Theme-word C* (9). *Variations:* 31 Dn. (5) and 17 (4)
34 State housing South American Men's Club (3)
37 Hydrogen weapon can cause injury . . . (4)
39 . . . or about the opposite (5)
41 Take back the bet—I may explode (4)

42 All ten ruined with anger (6)
43 To carve with hesitation is more dainty (5)
45 Purge from the East—so be it, from the East (5)
46 *Theme-word D* (8). *Variations:* 16 (5) and 5 (3)
47 What goes from the center to the edge in the Strad I use (6)
48 Considers an affront almost all the gifts (7)

DOWN

1 *Theme-word E* (5). *Variations:*

30 (5) and 12 Ac. (3)
2 Concerning the district income (7)
3 Oh, gosh, the moulding's like an S (4)
4 Water propeller sounds like the alternative (3)
6 Drinks all around might cause song (4)
7 Negative printed in brown-orange (3)
8 One with a lot of gossip (3)
9 Is unable to talk hypocritically (4)
10 Carol is to sing just as Morris is

to dance (7)
12 The last letter is in French relish (4)
15 Lean out of a gas-lantern (5)
19 Members of the ruling class use rash logic, being spoiled (9)
20 Left the role in the middle of the Act (8)
21 Laborer with nothing in prison (4)
22 This is a prison term. This is another. (8)
23 Write for someone else with spirit (5)
25 Ice gliders from

Sark, set in motion (7)
26 Half this is an idiot—all this is quite the reverse (3)
32 Dance from "The Spanish Hour" (4)
33 Hesitation in French-born musicin's note (5)
35 Concerning part of a permanent wave (5)
38 Does she stick on one note in "La Boheme"? (4)
40 Successor to "The Sound of Music" (4)
44 Heavy French fashion (3)

Instructions. The heavy bars in the diagram indicate the beginnings and ends of words, just as black squares do in the usual crossword puzzle. The numbers in parentheses at the end of each clue denote the number of letters in the "light" (the answer to be filled in).

In this puzzle, fifteen of the lights have no written clues: there are five Theme-words, A, B, C, D, and E, which form a familiar group with something in common. Each Theme-word has its own pair of "variations" with a certain relationship to it. The relationship is somewhat different in each case.

E.g., if Theme-word A were SALT, its variations might be SAILOR and TAR; and if Theme-word B were PEPPER, its variations might be VIM and THROUGH (pep = vim, per = through).

Ignore punctuation, which is designed to confuse.

SOLUTIONS

From *New York* Magazine

```
GIGA BALD  VISAS  POSSE
ORRS EGAN  ONICE  ACHES
WEOKMANYAZINGER  REARS
NNW  UKES  OLIN    LARVA
 EKES  WIZMANAGERONKEY
  ELEC NOB  GLOWERS
GUNBOAT NIAS  BAAS  ADO
ATYA DRAKES  SINS    RIP
MEA  DIOR   ISO   ORIENT
ERN  OZMYREAWAKENING
ROMEO  PAUL  APOD  VEILS
 AGREENMINKYOWZA  ZIP
ARIOSE  MAO   KOOL  AVE
ROZ   RACY  RUNYON  AMEN
TOE  MINH  DINO  DESCENT
  RELEASE  POL   DERN
GOZANYWINEMAKER  LEWD
ARENT   OPEC  NOTI  OOF
MOLTO  MYWEEKINORGANZA
UNDER  DEIST  ROSE  SKED
TOADS  CANTS  ANTE  HYDE
```

Solution to puzzle on page 4

Do I Hear a W?

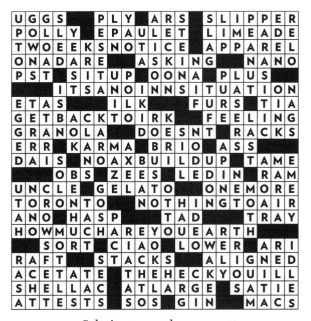

```
UGGS   PLY  ARS  SLIPPER
POLLY  EPAULET  LIMEADE
TWOEEKSNOTICE  APPAREL
ONADARE  ASKING   NANO
PST  SITUP  OONA  PLUS
  ITSANOINNSITUATION
ETAS   ILK   FURS   TIA
GETBACKTOIRK  FEELING
GRANOLA  DOESNT  RACKS
ERR  KARMA  BRIO  ASS
DAIS  NOAXBUILDUP  TAME
  OBS  ZEES  LEDIN  RAM
UNCLE  GELATO  ONEMORE
TORONTO  NOTHINGTOAIR
ANO  HASP   TAD   TRAY
HOWMUCHAREYOUEARTH
 SORT  CIAO  LOWER  ARI
RAFT   STACKS  ALIGNED
ACETATE  THEHECKYOUILL
SHELLAC  ATLARGE  SATIE
ATTESTS  SOS  GIN   MACS
```

Solution to puzzle on page 5

Wacky Weather

```
PAWS  ALBS   TRASH   URN
IRAE  SLEPT  MOVIES  TAE
LILT  HAVEANICEDAY  IVE
LETT   MECCA   RETRACED
SLEETTALKINGUY  ITALY
 REAR   START   LEAH
LOW  GIBB  SEEDED  OTTO
OMIT  PROSY   RING  SHAW
INNOREASTERBONNET  EXE
SIDLE  ENAMEL  TYRO  AID
 CLAP   REVUE   STAG
DUH  TOES  NERUDA  ABEAM
URI  ALLHAILBROKELOOSE
KALE  IBID   SONIC  OFIT
ELLA  COMMIT  SNOB  FAS
 SLEW  IDIOM   LEAR
TOMEI  ITSSNOWBIGDEAL
UNCLESAM  NODAL   VERA
LEG  TEMPESTFUGIT  IZOD
SUE  ORIENT  FLESH  SINE
APE   BEIGE   ESSO  ENID
```

Solution to puzzle on page 6

Sounds Like a Woman

```
SUAVE  ABBE  SAME  WISH
ASLEEP  TOUR  ABEL  INTO
REIGNOFTARA  YAWL  TSAR
ARTE  SORRY  ONCEACHITA
 TETRA  AVOID  AIDES
ALWAYSACHITA   ANTES
NORTE   TYPO  RUSSO
TWEETED  PAININTHERHEA
ZEN  EVENED  ADORE  EARL
 PEACE   GIG  ESPANOL
ASSET  OZONELEIA  UPDOS
SOOTHER  AOL   SKITS
ILIA  DANTE  OTHERS  RIO
FOLLOWTHELEDA  REDIALS
 PIELS  MEME   OMNES
 ALLEN   SIDEVIEWMIRA
STAIR  COOPT   INANE
TAKEAHEDDA  PALAU  ROMP
ARES  OLIO  THEENDISNIA
GIRT  SLUR  WIRY  ELECTS
ESSO  TOMS  ALOE   ODETS
```

Solution to puzzle on page 7

Dual-Purpose Creatures

```
E S T A   S C H W A   A P S E S   ■ K O S
X E R S   A R I E L   L A H T I   ■ K E P T
P R E S I D E N T I A L S E A L   ■ N A T O
O F F E N D E D   ■ N I T A   ■ S O N I C
■ ■ R T E S   M A K E A F A S T B U C K
H E S T O N   B U I L D   ■ D U E S   ■
A L I S T   V O T R E   P A D R E   ■ A P E
N I N   O H A R A   S P E L L I N G B E E
D O E R   I C I N G   E R E   ■ R E A L
I T W A S J U S T A F L U K E   W A L K S
■ T H O U   ■ M A V   ■ T R O T   ■ ■
M I S T Y   M O N E Y I N T H E K I T T Y
O P A L   ■ M A T   S A R A N   S I R E
T A K E A G A N D E R   B I N D S   P A S
E D S   S O N I A   E M O T E   P R I C E
■ H O B O   ■ S C O R E   B L A N K S
A P A I N I N T H E A S S   L E A F   ■
C A D R E   ■ R O M P   T O A S T E R S
R U L E   C H O K E S U P O N T H E B A T
I S I S   R E V E L   P A N E L   R O V E
D E B   ■ O X E Y E   S P I R E   S N I P
```

Solution to puzzle on page 8

Medicine's a Business

```
C O P T S   ■ B L A I R   I M A C   S C A R
A B R A M   ■ L O R N A   C A R O   U L N A
P E E K A B O O I C U   E D A M   M A I D
T Y P E S E T   ■ A N I M A L P H A R M A
■ ■ H A T E S   C R A M   L O C K E R
A S T I   M O R E T H A N   O A R   ■ ■
C L A S P   ■ T R O Y   S K I N C I T Y
N O M E A N F E E T   S A T A N   A S I A
E T E R N A L   A L L O Y   ■ F I L L Y
■ E T T A S   T R I A L   C A N A D A
R I M   H A P P Y E N T R A I L S   M A S
E N A M E L   R O T A S   F L A T S   ■
M A T E R   P E R E Z   ■ E R E C T E D
U N T O   P E A K S   N U T R A S U I T E
S E E W O R L D   ■ D O R A   T B O N E
■ V A T   A F I L L I N G   A S A P
O B T A I N   A C I D   S L O O P   ■
G L A N D C E N T R A L   O N E I D A S
L O N G   I S I S   W O M B S E R V I C E
E K G S   N A T O   A L I C E   K A R M A
R E S T   G I A N   Y A T E S   S N E E R
```

Solution to puzzle on page 9

The "More" the Merrier

```
P O P A R T   T S A R   G M T   B E R E T
O P I N E S   O T R A   E A R   O R A T E
C U T T H E C O R D S   T R U E G R I T S
O S H E A   I L I E   A C C R A   N U T
■ ■ B I G B A N G S T H E O R Y   ■
P E R S O N A   T E A   ■ S T E R E O
A L P E   W A R M   A L G A E   L I M A
M A I T R E   W O R K E D O N S P E C S
A N S A E   D R A T   N A S A L   L E I
J A C K S I N T H E B O X   C E A S E S
■ E T T A S   R A N   M A H E R   ■
A M A N D A   L I T T L E B O P E E P S
S O O   A L A M O   A I D E   E A G E R
S O R R Y O L D C H A P S   A R R A N T
E S T A   S C I O N   A S E C   U L N A
T E A R U P   S K A   T R I A G E S
■ A R O U N D T H E B E N D S   ■
M O E   G O S E E   R O V E   K A N G A
A T T H E H O P S   H I V E S O F B E E S
S T A I N   F A A   M A I N   R O B E R T
T O L E T   A L I   O L D S   G R A D E A
```

Solution to puzzle on page 10

Describe the Clues

```
S C A M   H U L K   A B A S H   H I S S
E L L E   A R I E S   P A S E O   I D L E
W I L D A N I M A L   T R E N T   B E A T
S P Y I N G   E T A L   B A D B R E A T H
■ ■ A D A R   S T E P   ■ E E R   ■
B A R T E R E D   E X O T I C D A N C E R
A L O E S   L I U   S A R I   D I O D E
S A G S   W A N D A   S T A L E   A R S E
T R U   M I X E D B L E S S I N G   R E V
E M E R I L   R E B A   A S A R U L E
■ N A S H   O R A C L E S   U T E P   ■
F L A S H E S   E A S E   R E N T E D
R A T   A L T E R E D S T A T E S   F L A
I R I S   M I L L R   S O L I D   M I D I
A V O I D   E S A U   P E R   P O L E S
R A N D O M S A M P L E   R E F I N E R Y
■ E R A   T A L C   D R N O   ■
R O C K Y R O A D   B E A N   A C T U A L
A M O I   R A N U P   C R A Z Y H O R S E
N A R C   O T T E R   T E P E E   N A T S
T R E K   W H I T E   T E N D   E L I S
```

Solution to puzzle on page 11

Oldies Remixes

```
ANTES  STRUM  MAAM   FRET
LEONA  ARENA  AMMO   IOWA
TANGLEDUPINBLUEVELVET
OTT  AVA    GOAL   INTERS
SHOWMETHEWAYWEWERE
    AIR  EPI  ZITI  ARMED
ELAN     YELP    NAG  AMO
DOCTORMYEYESADOREDYOU
AGE  VISAS  ETTA  IDIOTS
MOD  ALG    LETUP    TREE
    LETITBEMYBABY
ARAB    SCOLD    BRA  RON
SELECT  OTTO  NOSIR  ICE
TELLHERNOSUGARTONIGHT
EVA  EAU    TUBS    BASS
REHEM  SOHO  LOO   CTA
    TIGHTENUPONTHEROOF
LAMESA  ILES    EAT  MRI
SHORTPEOPLEARESTRANGE
ASSN   ELSE  ROBOT  APIAN
TOTE   DOER  SKINS  STAND
```

Solution to puzzle on page 12

Fool's Paradise

```
BACH   ARCANA  WHO   AMIE
ELLA   GOADED  ROAR  MANN
GEORGEWBUSH   ETTU   BITE
GUSTO    OLSENS    GAINER
ATE  TRITT  RUTGERS  ING
RST  MAS    JESSICATANDY
    DEFACTO      ACTING
SPAR  TOUCHSTONE    GRIM
HARE     TUNEIN   APIECE
ILE  WOKE    EMO  SPEEDER
MET  ALEXANDERPOPE   IDI
MAHONEY  BEI   ASSN   ETD
ELANDS    ELEVEN    KNEE
REFI    WILLROGERS  ATAN
    ROSSES     NOSIEST
FRANKIELYMON   JET   ESP
EEN  APPEASE  DANNO   LEA
TAKETH    TSURIS   ODORS
IDLY  OPUS  VIVIENLEIGH
STIR  NOME  ROADIE  ASIA
HONE   WAN  ESSENE  LEOS
```

Solution to puzzle on page 13

Car-pun-try

```
ACMES  PRAM   IMAGE  CAPT
SHINE  HORA   DONOR  OLIO
HONDAJOBTRAINING   BILL
EPISTLE   TROTS   RABAT
    SONGSINTHEKIALIFE
MULE   IRENE     OMIT
ABUT  EXIT  RASCAL   EAU
RETAIL  SAABWITHCAMELS
CRESCENT  QUERY   TULIP
    ECO  AUF  ILSA  NETS
AINTTHATAFINEAUDIDO
ANNA  SOSO  ALG    IRA
PIETA   INALL  SLOVAKIA
PORSCHEDEROSSI   REGION
TNT  TALESE   HERA  ALTO
    EURO    ECONO   ROAN
MAZDAPIECETHEATRE
EMAIL   BALTO   AUTOMAT
WAIT  THEJEEPDETECTIVE
ETRE  RERUN  RILE  HIREE
DIED  AETNA  AXIS  ACORN
```

Solution to puzzle on page 14

Devilish Demonyms

```
GBS   TALC   TOTAL  WAFERS
OAT   AREA   AMORE  EVADES
THEGRANDKENYAN    BAREST
HARS  MIEN   IDI   STINTS
SINKSINTOABOLIVIAN
    KOS    CHUG  RETRACTS
TOOL   UKES   LORE    LEO
JIB  ODESSA  NINASAMOAN
ODE  SIMI   DOOMS   GODLY
GASP  DENT   TAI    STEM
SLEEPINGWITHTHEYEMENI
    RAND  ERE  SOAP  YEAS
ABNER   MEARA  UTES   RNA
PLAZASWEDE  LESSOR   INN
OUT   TIDY  GIVE    TREY
PROSPERO  URGE    MAO
    THENCANONLYKOSOVAR
PATROL  WSW  YEAR   SOME
ELAINE  TANNINGLAOTIAN
COPPER  BRAUN  GELD   DIA
STEEDS  DEPPS  SLED   SNL
```

Solution to puzzle on page 15

Literary Mash-ups

Solution to puzzle on page 16

Prefix Mix-ups

Solution to puzzle on page 17

Product Placement

Solution to puzzle on page 18

First World Problems

Solution to puzzle on page 19

Stuffed!

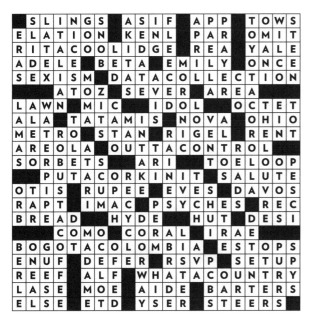

Solution to puzzle on page 20

Have ING Fun

Solution to puzzle on page 21

Likely Excuses

Solution to puzzle on page 22

Turnabout Is Fair Play

Solution to puzzle on page 23

Broadway Runs

Solution to puzzle on page 24

For Fun

Solution to puzzle on page 25

MediCine

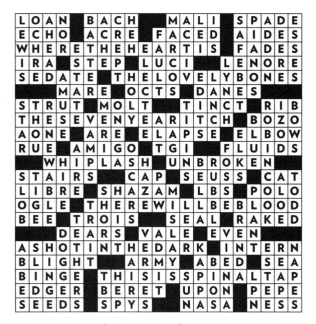

Solution to puzzle on page 26

Med School Caper

Solution to puzzle on page 27

Letter Play

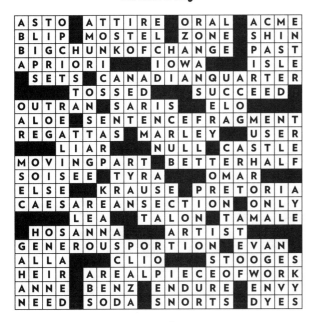

A	S	T	O		A	T	T	I	R	E		O	R	A	L		A	C	M	E
B	L	I	P		M	O	S	T	E	L		Z	O	N	E		S	H	I	N
B	I	G	C	H	U	N	K	O	F	C	H	A	N	G	E		P	A	S	T
A	P	R	I	O	R	I		I	O	W	A		I	S	L	E
	S	E	T	S		C	A	N	A	D	I	A	N	Q	U	A	R	T	E	R
		T	O	S	S	E	D			S	U	C	C	E	E	D
O	U	T	R	A	N		S	A	R	I	S		E	L	O
A	L	O	E		S	E	N	T	E	N	C	E	F	R	A	G	M	E	N	T
R	E	G	A	T	T	A	S		M	A	R	L	E	Y		U	S	E	R
	L	I	A	R		N	U	L	L		C	A	S	T	L	E
M	O	V	I	N	G	P	A	R	T		B	E	T	T	E	R	H	A	L	F
S	O	I	S	E	E		T	Y	R	A		O	M	A	R
E	L	S	E		K	R	A	U	S	E		P	R	E	T	O	R	I	A
C	A	E	S	A	R	E	A	N	S	E	C	T	I	O	N		O	N	L	Y
	L	E	A		T	A	L	O	N		T	A	M	A	L	E
	H	O	S	A	N	N	A			A	R	T	I	S	T
G	E	N	E	R	O	U	S	P	O	R	T	I	O	N		E	V	A	N
A	L	L	A		C	L	I	O			S	T	O	O	G	E	S
H	E	I	R		A	R	E	A	L	P	I	E	C	E	O	F	W	O	R	K
A	N	N	E		B	E	N	Z		E	N	D	U	R	E		E	N	V	Y
N	E	E	D		S	O	D	A		S	N	O	R	T	S		D	Y	E	S

Solution to puzzle on page 28

Wear to Eat

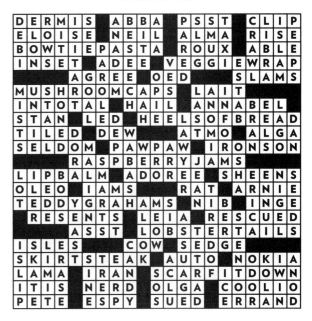

D	E	R	M	I	S		A	B	B	A		P	S	S	T		C	L	I	P
E	L	O	I	S	E		N	E	I	L		A	L	M	A		R	I	S	E
B	O	W	T	I	E	P	A	S	T	A		R	O	U	X		A	B	L	E
I	N	S	E	T		A	D	E	E		V	E	G	G	I	E	W	R	A	P
			A	G	R	E	E		O	E	D		S	L	A	M	S
M	U	S	H	R	O	O	M	C	A	P	S		L	A	I	T
I	N	T	O	T	A	L		H	A	I	L		A	N	N	A	B	E	L
S	T	A	N		L	E	D		H	E	E	L	S	O	F	B	R	E	A	D
T	I	L	E	D		D	E	W			A	T	M	O		A	L	G	A
S	E	L	D	O	M		P	A	W	P	A	W		I	R	O	N	S	O	N
			R	A	S	P	B	E	R	R	Y	J	A	M	S
L	I	P	B	A	L	M		A	D	O	R	E	E		S	H	E	E	N	S
O	L	E	O		I	A	M	S		R	A	T		A	R	N	I	E
T	E	D	D	Y	G	R	A	H	A	M	S		N	I	B		I	N	G	E
	R	E	S	E	N	T	S		L	E	I	A		R	E	S	C	U	E	D
		A	S	S	T		L	O	B	S	T	E	R	T	A	I	L	S
I	S	L	E	S			C	O	W		S	E	D	G	E
S	K	I	R	T	S	T	E	A	K		A	U	T	O		N	O	K	I	A
L	A	M	A		I	R	A	N		S	C	A	R	F	I	T	D	O	W	N
I	T	I	S		N	E	R	D		O	L	G	A		C	O	O	L	I	O
P	E	T	E		E	S	P	Y		S	U	E	D		E	R	R	A	N	D

Solution to puzzle on page 29

Bollywood Titles

P	E	L	T		S	P	A	R		M	A	N	N	S		T	A	S	S	E
O	T	O	E		A	O	N	E		T	R	A	C	I		I	S	L	A	M
O	N	C	E	U	P	O	N	A	M	A	D	R	A	S		R	E	A	L	M
F	A	K	I	R		R	A	G	E		C	A	S	T	E	A	W	A	Y
	S	E	N	D	E	E		A	L	I	T		Y	A	W
		G	U	Y	S	A	N	D	D	A	L	S		P	E	S	T	S
S	C	I		E	T	S		I	B	E	A	M		A	O	R	T	A
P	E	N	T	A	D		T	A	N	D	O	O	R	M	E	R	C	I	E	S
O	C	T	E	T		Z	U	L	U		O	S	A	M	A		M	E	A
T	E	R	R	A		A	T	I	M	E			R	Y	D	E	R	S
	A	P	R	I	C	E	A	B	O	V	E	R	U	P	E	E	S
R	U	S	S	I	A			S	E	R	U	M		A	L	T	E	R
O	N	T		M	I	L	E	S		R	O	M	P		S	T	E	V	E
W	H	A	T	A	B	O	U	T	K	A	B	O	B		S	T	A	R	E	D
S	I	T	A	R		U	N	T	I	L		L	A	O		S	R	S
	P	E	R	M	S		K	A	R	M	A	G	E	D	D	O	N
		B	Y	E		T	A	P	A		P	A	G	O	D	A
R	A	J	A	A	N	D	M	E		E	L	I	A		P	R	O	V	O
A	L	I	G	N		S	A	R	I	W	R	O	N	G	N	U	M	B	E	R
C	A	V	E	D		E	L	A	T	E		O	R	E	O		A	I	R	E
K	N	E	E	S		L	I	S	T	S		T	E	S	T		L	E	S	S

Solution to puzzle on page 30

Speak-k Easy

D	O	R	M		V	A	L	E		A	R	E	S		S	H	A	L	E
A	C	E	D		E	V	A	N	S		S	E	M	I		T	O	N	E	D
T	H	I	S	I	S	A	S	T	I	C	K	C	U	P		E	M	E	N	D
E	E	K		R	I	I	S		S	O	O		L	E	E	W	A	Y
D	R	I	N	K	C	L	O	T	S	O	F	F	L	U	I	D	S
		I	S	L	E		A	Y	N		R	O	L	L	S		F	A	O
P	L	A	N		E	D	E	R		I	O	N	A		S	L	I	M
A	I	D	E			B	A	D	S	T	O	M	A	C	H	C	A	K	E
T	E	A		A	L	A	I		R	E	O		A	L	I	E	N
H	U	M	P	B	A	C	K	Q	U	A	I	L		T	A	V	E	R	N	S
		O	R	O	M	E	O			E	R	A	S	E	R
A	M	B	R	O	S	E		M	A	K	E	K	I	T	S	N	A	P	P	Y
M	O	T	T	O			L	I	P		N	A	T	S		L	O	U
B	R	E	A	K	K	I	N	P	E	R	I	O	D		G	A	L	L
E	T	A	L		H	O	S	E		P	S	S	T		L	Y	L	E
R	E	M		S	A	N	E	R		I	C	E		C	A	P	O
	L	I	K	E	C	U	S	S	O	N	F	A	C	E	B	O	O	K
S	A	L	A	M	I			P	A	N		E	R	T	E		L	S	U
A	L	I	B	I		S	T	A	R	K	C	R	A	V	I	N	G	M	A	D
G	I	M	E	L		H	U	L	A		H	O	T	E	L		L	A	G	O
S	T	O	L	E		E	X	I	T			E	S	S	E		O	N	E	S

Solution to puzzle on page 31

Tiger Mother

```
I R T   T A O   B A L O O   A L K A L I
D O A   T O I L   A L A N S   D E E D E D
E A R N O U R S T R I P E S   V A N D A L
A N T E U P   E R R A T A   F A D   S K Y
      G R E E N E   O C T A N E
  T E A S E L   B E U P T O S C R A T C H
S I L T   C O L O N S   R T E   D O H A
H A V E C H I N E S E   B I B S   A R I D
I R E   R O D E   T U N A   A L I
V A S S A R   G O I N G T O C A T C H I T
    A W E S   P O S I T   K E E P
Y O U L L B E S T U F F E D   S M U T T Y
A N N   R A E S   A P O P   O R O
R E I D   A V I D   C U B R E P O R T E R
D A T E   N A N   R O S I E R   E I N E
S L E E P I N T H E D E N   P A D D E D
    E S T E E M   G A S T R O
S P A   D E S   R O M P E R   T E A S E S
T O M C A T   G A V E U S A L I C K I N G
A N O I N T   O L E A N   B E C K   L I T
B E R A T E   O D D L Y   S E A   O D S
```

Solution to puzzle on page 32

Wherever You Go

```
O N D I S C   O R A N G S   E C L I P S E
B O R N E O   N O S A L E   C O U R I E R
S H A K I N G M Y H E A D   H O B O K E N
  O W S   T H E S E   C A N O P E N E R S
    T O R I   P I N E   E R S T
A N G E L A   T I A R A   T R E A D
C O R R E C T I O N A L   O R R   B A A
I N E   T U R N I N   P O T O F G O L D
D E E M S   L E A   C R I M E S   R O O D
S T R E E P S   G E E S E   I C A R U S
    W C H A N D Y   V A N L O O S
M O J I T O   A U R A S   O N E S T O P
A M I N   T R A D E S   M S G   N O R S E
L O N G J O H N S   T R O P I C   A S A
L O X   E O E   P R I V Y C O U N C I L
    A T P A R   R I C E S   A G A T E S
A M O K   B R E D   R U H R
F A C I L I T I E S   T R A I T   R A H
T I T M I C E   G A M E O F T H R O N E S
E N A B L E S   A G E N D A   O N W A R D
R E L O A D S   L E T T E R   R A S T A S
```

Solution to puzzle on page 33

Au Pairs

```
G O O D   G E S S O   A H E M   C L O D
O M N I   M A N A N A   D E L I   E E R O
G A U G E S P A G E S   D I L L   T S A R
O N S E T   R E A L M   G I A M A T T I
    S T A F F S L A U G H S   I C E E S
V E N T U R A   P R A T   S T E R
E G O   I N E R T   P T S   C R A W L S
G A U C H O G R O U C H O   T O E N A I L
A N N I E S   A L L A Y   E R R S   N E O
    T A O S   L I P   S P I N   M T G E
B E R E T   T A U P E S O A P   M O S E S
A X E D   S I M P   L P N   E D E N
T I S   I K E A   B L O A T   O N E D G E
E S T A D O S   B E A U T Y S C U T I E S
S T A R E S   S R A   T A R O T   O R T
  U T A H   C O R P   L O W E R E D
E G R E T   T A W D R Y A U D R E Y
F L A R E D U P   S E A R S   A E T N A
R A N I   A B U T   P R O N O U N C E A U
E R T E   R E L O   S I M O N E   U L A N
M E S S   T R A Y   S A T A Y   P E N T
```

Solution to puzzle on page 34

Guys' Guise

```
N O I D E A   A N N U M   R E D S   O N T
A S S E N T   L E O N A   O R A L   N E O
P H I L H A R M O N I C   T O M A H A W K
S A S H A   E O N S   R U T S   B U B B E
  I N C A S   T E A S E   R E I N
O R B   C U R T A I L M E N T   D O T E S
T O I L E R   A C M E   E V E N
I S L A   S P A R K S   C A R O M   S P A
C A L M   E R I E   A L T R U I S T I C
  A P O D A L   C O M E T   S L O U G H
G A B O N   M E L O D I O U S   L A P S E
O T O O L E   R O O D S   N U M E R O
D O N N Y B R O O K   T E R A   E R I N
S I G   Y O U N T   G I R D E R   R O L O
    S O N S   B A R I   I S S U E S
S H A M U   T H E O L O G I C A L   S A Y
T A M A   O L D E N   M I N O R
E L E C T   I C K Y   B O O T   T E A M S
R I C K R A C K   F R A N K I N C E N S E
N T H   O B O E   A T R I A   E A S T E R
S E E   D E N Y   T E S T Y   G R E E C E
```

Solution to puzzle on page 35

Film Splices

Solution to puzzle on page 36

A Separate Piece

Solution to puzzle on page 37

Extra Syllable, Puh-lease

```
A D A R   K E E P S   W E L L   P S A T
N O N E   O N S E T   E R I E   O P R A H
T W O B A R O Q U E G I R L S   T R I B E
I N M A T E     F O G     S E R I A L S
  A T T A C K O F T H E C O L O G N E S
H A L E Y   O M N I     T O N K A
A M I S   C L A M   S H O T     S C A L A
R O E   T H O R E A U I N T H E T O W E L
M I S P R I N T   P E N   O U T   R E A P
    R A P   W E D D I N G D U R E S S
  L A O S   C H I     D Y E   M A K E
N E D P H I L A N D E R S     S I L
A C R O   S U I   I D O   T R E A S U R E
S H E S A T E R R A I N W R E C K   P A X
H E M E N   O U S T   C A M O   D I N E
    E D D I E     A T M O   B E N D S
W I D E W O R L D O F S U P P O R T S
A V O N L E A   S A C     P E R M I T
D A N T E   W O R K Y O U R G A L O O T S
E N N E A   U L N A   T R I A L   I K E A
  S E R F   P E A R   S N O B S   T E R R
```

Solution to puzzle on page 38

Heard Mentality

```
S A B R E   O D D   A G R A   R E B A T E
A L I E N   R A Y   L O U D   E L I S H A
H I G H G R A Y E D B O N D   S I S T E R
L A D E   A T A R I   D E I S T   T I M E
      A S P E N   S W I S S C H A R R E D
S E C R E T S   O P I E     H O B O
A B U S E   A V E R S   A M M O   B A A
G O R E D F A M I L Y   M O O E D R I N G
E N D   E R R E D   M A L   E E R I E
    B R A I N   R O O K   R E S E C T S
  S A O   M A D E O F H O N O R   F H A
E N D U R E S   B A T S   A S I C S
L O R N E   L A D   C I S C O   A R I
O W E D T O J O Y   I T A L I A N B R E D
I S M   U R A L   C O V E S   F A T A L
    T R I M   O N I N   S C E N E R Y
S T R I N G B A N N E D   S H A R D
C H I N   I S L E S   O C E A N   A S H E
R E G I O N   T H E B L I N D S I G H E D
A T H E N A   O I N K   T S E   D E E R E
P A T R O L   S S T S   Y E S   A D D O N
```

Solution to puzzle on page 39

Pun-itive Diet

Solution to puzzle on page 40

A Game of Motto

Solution to puzzle on page 41

Think in Initials

Solution to puzzle on page 42

Part Latin

Solution to puzzle on page 43

Vowel Swaps

```
L O F T  ▓ A C H E D ▓ M A C S ▓ A M I S
O M A H A ▓ G U I D E ▓ I D L Y ▓ K A N T
T A X E S H O L D E M ▓ N O O N ▓ A N T E
U N E A S Y ▓ P E N A L T R U C K ▓ T O V
S I D ▓ E A T A ▓ ▓ R A Z E D ▓ L O E W E
▓ ▓ R S T U ▓ A R C H ▓ ▓ S P E L L ▓ ▓
C H R I S T M A S C O R A L ▓ R E D H O T
R E E V E S ▓ S P A ▓ ▓ V I T A ▓ S E R A
U M P E D ▓ S E E ▓ ▓ H E L E N A ▓ A L P
S P U R ▓ S C A R E T I C T A C S ▓ L Y E
▓ ▓ B A S T A ▓ T A R ▓ ▓ R E A C T ▓ ▓
L I L ▓ C A R P E T B E G G A R ▓ R H E O
I D I ▓ I T A L I A ▓ R O T ▓ W I D T H
M O C K ▓ U B E R ▓ F I B ▓ C A M A R O
B L O N D E ▓ B E T T E D I V A S E Y E S
▓ F E A S T ▓ ▓ H E N S ▓ A G H A ▓ ▓
L I K E S ▓ S T O O L ▓ U N I T ▓ S A C
I D A ▓ H E H A S R E S I N ▓ E U R O P A
B I N S ▓ W I L T ▓ C O S T A R B E A N S
Y O Y O ▓ E R I E ▓ O L L I E ▓ S P R E E
A M E X ▓ S T A R ▓ M E A L S ▓ O S A Y
```

Solution to puzzle on page 44

Griddy Sounds

```
A R R O W ▓ E V E ▓ S T A L L ▓ D R A M A
L E I C A ▓ N I B ▓ Y A L I E ▓ E A T E R
O F F T R A C K B E D D I N G ▓ S P R E E
W I F E ▓ P O K E R ▓ S E A T S ▓ I K E
▓ ▓ T H E R I D I N G O N T H E W A L L
C U P ▓ E S E ▓ S U N ▓ E E R I L Y ▓ ▓
O Z O N E ▓ ▓ S A V E S ▓ B E E T S ▓ ▓
T I D A L C H A R A C T E R ▓ ▓ E A S E
E S S O ▓ A A R O N ▓ S H U D D E R B U G
▓ ▓ M A N S I O N S ▓ S T E E D ▓ A L A
C A S I N O S ▓ A I R ▓ ▓ A M I S T A D
O J O ▓ E L I H U ▓ T A B U L A T E ▓ ▓
C A L L W A D I N G ▓ M A V E N ▓ A T O Z
O R E O ▓ ▓ Y O U R E H E R D I N G M E
▓ C A R T A ▓ M E N S A ▓ A S I A N ▓ ▓
▓ D R A P E R ▓ A B E ▓ L A G ▓ F R O
D I A L O G U E S O F P L A Y D O H ▓ ▓
O T T ▓ S O M N I ▓ A O R T A ▓ A P S E
W H I S T ▓ P U D D I N O N T H E R I T Z
S E O U L ▓ E R E C T ▓ T I O ▓ P E T E R
E R N I E ▓ T E S L A ▓ S E N ▓ A M A N A
```

Solution to puzzle on page 45

Comic Con

```
A A N D W ▓ A C M E S ▓ A S P S ▓ S A R I
S T I E S ▓ R O O S T ▓ S H A H ▓ I B I D
C O N F U S I O N C U I S I N E ▓ P I P E
O N E A ▓ W A T T ▓ V A R I ▓ ▓ L E A
T A T T O O ▓ ▓ H O T A I R C O N V E N T
S L Y ▓ B R A C ▓ W A N ▓ ▓ L I E N E E
▓ ▓ C O N F O U N D I N G F A T H E R S
I N G L E ▓ T S P S ▓ ▓ O L I V E ▓ ▓
N O L A ▓ P O E T ▓ F U T O N ▓ C O P
F O U R C O N C O U R S E M E A L ▓ A V E
E S T A D O ▓ ▓ B A M ▓ R E A M E R ▓ ▓
C E E ▓ C H I C K E N C O N T E N D E R S
T D S ▓ ▓ T I E R S ▓ R A E S ▓ D O D O
▓ ▓ L A I N E ▓ A I N T ▓ M E S O N ▓ ▓
C O N D E S C E N D I N G O R D E R ▓ ▓
E L E C T S ▓ ▓ E C O ▓ S A Y S ▓ P R O
N O W C O N S E R V I N G ▓ L A G O O N
T R Y ▓ O L E O ▓ I S T A ▓ O P U S
R O E S ▓ I S L A N D O F C O N C R E T E
I S A K ▓ P A I D ▓ O N T A P ▓ A S Y E T
C O R A ▓ O D E S ▓ C O S M O ▓ R E E D S
```

Solution to puzzle on page 46

Thanksgiving Leftovers

```
W H E L P ▓ A R U B A ▓ T E R N ▓ E P P S
A O L E R ▓ M I L E Y ▓ A L P O ▓ S U E T
G R A V E N I M A G E ▓ O L I V E T R E E
S O N A T A ▓ ▓ N I S I ▓ ▓ T A S T E
▓ ▓ R E B U S ▓ N I C E C O L D B E E R
A S T ▓ N O T T O ▓ R E G A R D S ▓ ▓
C L O U D B U R S T ▓ B A R D S ▓ M I R A
H O W L S ▓ R E A R ▓ A L O E ▓ S A V E S
E P E E ▓ S N A K I N G ▓ B R A T P A C K
S E L E N A ▓ M A N E ▓ ▓ E R R A N D S
▓ ▓ O B S ▓ N A M U R ▓ D E I ▓ ▓
I N S T O R E ▓ E L E V ▓ N A U G H T
L E A R N E R S ▓ H A N D O U T ▓ G L O W
Y A L I E ▓ A T N O ▓ A T I P ▓ C L O N E
A R E S ▓ A P I A N ▓ R A C E D R I V E R
▓ A G E L E S S ▓ G E N R E ▓ E S T
Y O U R B E S T S H O T ▓ S N O W S ▓ ▓
A R N I E ▓ ▓ U N O S ▓ ▓ O N E O F F
S O I L S T A I N ▓ O P E N A L E T T E R
I N T L ▓ R U L E ▓ M I M E S ▓ C O R E A
R O S S ▓ E X E S ▓ A C I D S ▓ K N O T S
```

Solution to puzzle on page 47

The message, made up of the 18 first letters from the theme answers, is COUNT YOUR BLESSINGS

Season to Be Punny

Solution to puzzle on page 48

You Get an A!

Solution to puzzle on page 49

Split Seconds

Solution to puzzle on page 50

Bad Hair-Pun Day

Solution to puzzle on page 51

Project Roadway

A	B	A	C	I			N	A	E	S		D	E	W	Y		W	I	S	E
S	E	R	E	N	A		O	R	N	O		O	C	H	O		I	D	E	S
S	T	I	C	K	S	H	I	F	T	S		C	L	A	Y		T	I	N	T
A	S	S	E	S	S	E	S		R	A	D	I	A	T	O	R	H	O	S	E
D	Y	E			E	X	O	D		E	L	I			A	I	M	E	E	
		P	U	T	A	M	U	F	F	L	E	R	O	N	I	T				
K	A	R	E	L			E	E	R	O			T	I	S		H	A	S	
E	P	A	U	L	E	T		T	O	P	O	F	F	T	H	E	T	A	N	K
D	I	I		M	A	R	C	O	S		A	R	L	O		S	E	I	N	E
S	A	N	M	A	T	E	O		C	H	O	O			P	R	O	D		
	D	O	N		F	U	E	L	P	U	M	P	S		M	I	L			
M	I	R	O			R	A	I	L		P	A	R	A	D	I	S	E		
O	Z	O	N	E		F	I	R	E		S	T	Y	L	E	D		N	I	A
P	O	P	S	T	H	E	C	L	U	T	C	H		E	L	E	V	E	N	S
E	D	S		O	I	L			A	U	R	A			U	P	S	E	T	
			D	I	S	T	R	I	B	U	T	O	R	C	A	P	S			
A	R	E	E	L		E	N	E		B	R	A	M		S	A	D			
J	U	M	P	E	R	C	A	B	L	E	S		I	D	E	A	L	I	Z	E
O	B	I	E		A	R	G	O		C	H	E	V	Y	B	L	A	Z	E	R
K	I	L	N		S	E	A	R		H	O	R	A		A	D	V	E	R	B
E	K	E	D		P	E	N	N		O	P	A	L		A	S	S	A	Y	

Solution to puzzle on page 52

It's How You Say It

J	E	T	S		S	E	P	T	A		T	R	E	N	T		B	A	A	L
I	D	O	L		N	O	R	A	D		S	E	L	A	H		A	F	R	O
M	I	N	U	T	E	M	A	I	D		O	F	F	P	U	T	T	I	N	G
S	T	Y	M	I	E		I	L	E	R		I	P	S	E		R	I	O	
			G	R	A	S		N	O	T	O	N	E		F	L	E	E	S	
G	E	T	T	H	E	L	E	A	D	O	U	T		D	E	L	I			
E	L	A	N	T	R	A		W	A	S	S	E	R		L	O	P	E	S	
S	I	L	O		S	C	A	N		T	H	R	E	E	I	N	A	R	O	W
S	A	L	T		K	N	I	T		I	N	S	T		R	I	P	E		
O	N	S	E	T	S		I	N	A	N	E		A	I	R	I	E	S	T	
			B	A	S	S	G	U	I	T	A	R	I	S	T				
R	E	I	S	S	U	E		S	P	A	D	E		M	E	D	I	A	N	
A	R	A	M		C	N	B	C		L	O	N	G		I	N	C	A		
N	O	M	O	R	E	T	E	A	R	S		B	E	E	P		A	L	U	M
O	S	K	A	R		T	R	A	N	C	E		N	E	O	N	A	T	E	
E	S	S	O		D	R	E	S	S	E	R	D	R	A	W	E	R		
M	A	R	S	H		U	N	S	E	A	L		V	E	I	L				
E	D	O		E	A	T	A		K	E	N	O		C	O	E	R	C	E	
S	E	W	E	R	P	I	P	E	S		W	I	N	D	U	P	T	O	Y	S
S	L	A	T		S	E	E	K	S		I	N	N	E	R		R	O	S	A
Y	E	N	S		E	S	S	E	N		S	E	E	M	E		E	T	T	U

Solution to puzzle on page 53

Solution to puzzle on page 55

HIGHBROW. LOWBROW.
BRILLIANT. DESPICABLE.
50 YEARS of

New York

By the Editors of
NEW YORK MAGAZINE

**Available
wherever books
are sold or at**

SIMONANDSCHUSTER.COM